MANY FACES, MANY VOICES

MULTICULTURAL LITERARY
EXPERIENCES FOR YOUTH

MANY FACES, MANY VOICES

MULTICULTURAL LITERARY EXPERIENCES FOR YOUTH

THE VIRGINIA HAMILTON CONFERENCE

Edited by
Anthony L. Manna and Carolyn S. Brodie

Kent State University

Highsmith
PRESS

Fort Atkinson, Wisconsin

Published by Highsmith Press
W5527 Highway 106
P.O. Box 800
Fort Atkinson, Wisconsin 53538-0800

The paper used in this publication meets the minimum requirements of American
National Standard for Information Science — Permanence of Paper for Printed Library
Material. ANSI/NISO Z39.48-1984.

Library of Congress Cataloging in Publication

Many faces, many voices : multicultural literary experiences for youth : the
Virginia Hamilton Conference / edited by Anthony L. Manna and Carolyn S.
Brodie.
     p. cm.
   ISBN 0-917846-12-5 (alk. paper) : $29.00
    1. Children's literature, American--History and criticism--Congresses.
2. Children--United States--Books and reading--Congresses. 3. Pluralism (Social
sciences) in literature--Congresses. 4. Ethnic groups in literature--Congresses.
I. Manna, Anthony L. II. Brodie, Carolyn S., 1958-   .
PS490.M36 1992
810.9'9282--dc20   92-31119
                                                                                                    CIP

ISBN 0-917846-12-5

IN MEMORY OF CLARA O. JACKSON

The past moves me and with me, although I remove myself from it. It's light often shines on this night traveler: and when it does, I scribble it down. Whatever pleasure is in it I need pass on. That's happiness. That is who I am.

Virginia Hamilton

CONTENTS

FOREWORD

In the early 1980s, the late Clara Jackson, Professor Emeritus at Kent State University, School of Library Science, and Anthony Manna and others began talking about instituting a conference at the University that would attract teachers and librarians from the region. The primary emphasis of the conference would be the literature contributed by writers and illustrators of ethnic, parallel culture communities—African American, Asian American, Hispanic, Jewish, etc. The conference would provide a balanced view of the wide range of cultural, artistic, and literary development in literature for children and young adults.

My husband, Arnold Adoff, and I knew Clara Jackson many years before the founding of this conference on multicultural literature. She was an early supporter of our work when we first began publishing in the 1960s. She had presented the work of other parallel culture writers as well as our own in her courses, and at previous conferences at the Kent State Library School. Clara and her husband, Gabe, both librarians and professors, came from an active intellectual New York community, dating back to the 1930s, that had a strong commitment to presenting the multiple realities of American literature beyond the usual tokenism then found in textbooks and academic courses.

When Clara Jackson expanded her library science programs to include the work of Dr. Manna and others at the College of Education and the general liberal arts program, she was attempting to integrate the study of children's literature into the broadest range of academic disciplines, and to introduce it to the widest community participation of teachers, librarians, and parents.

By the late 1970s and 1980s, I had expanded my own work for young people in the area of fiction, to include nonfiction, biographies of the great black scholar, W. E. B. DuBois, and the extraordinary baritone singer and social activist, Paul Robeson.

When Clara Jackson contacted me about her proposed multicultural conference in my name at Kent State, I was continuing my literary work in what I term Liberation Literature—the literature of trial and struggle to freedom, through which the reader bears witness to the tribulation and ultimate deliverance, thus becoming liberated as well. The Liberation Literature work, *The People Could Fly: American Black Folktales* (Knopf, 1985), became a landmark folktale collection of Plantation Era folklore. Another such work of mine, *Anthony Burns: The Defeat and Triumph of a Fugitive Slave* (Knopf, 1988) is an award-winning historical reconstruction of the life of an actual slave who became a fugitive and finally a free man.

It seemed natural that I would lend my name to the Kent State conference. I felt proud to have been asked to join with educators in expanding the scope of multicultural literature.

Nineteen ninety-three will mark the ninth annual Virginia Hamilton Conference on Multicultural Literary Experiences for Youth. The yearly conference has grown to national status. It is today the pioneer and premier conference in literary and academic practice focusing on multiculturalism. I am amazed at how quickly it has reached audience capacity, as teachers, public librarians, school librarians, students of children's literature, writers, illustrators, parents, workshop presenters of related subjects, come eagerly each spring from across the country to attend and participate.

America is for me a country of parallel cultures rather than the more traditional, narrower view that portrays it as a land of the majority surrounded by minorities. It is a country of parallel peoples, each creating a significant literature out of their own unique yet universal qualities. Therefore, it must be a land where all cultures and all ethnic groups are of equal value and of equal importance to our children, who are descendents of the world's peoples. The Virginia Hamilton Conference promotes the vital work of enlarging understanding of the realities of American multicultural life and literature.

I am personally very gratified that previous proceedings of the conference are now being published by Highsmith Press in this first volume, *Many Faces, Many Voices*. This publication will open wide windows of scholarship and intellectual endeavor to an even greater national audience. We look forward to many conferences and Highsmith collections.

VIRGINIA HAMILTON

PREFACE

In 1983, several of us at Kent State University came together to discuss the possibility of establishing a conference that would focus exclusively on cultural diversity in literature for young people. Crossing the boundries of our respective academic disciplines—library and information science, education, and English—we discussed our mutual concerns, and often expressed our dismay about the types of cultural experiences, images, and attitudes which authors and illustrators of children's books convey to young people.

What evolved from these initial meetings was a commitment to creating a conference which would reflect and capture the tone of our own spirited debate and conversations. We wanted this conference to take the shape of a forum where authors, illustrators, school and public librarians, educators, critics, and others who work with children and children's books in any capacity could explore literature and other arts which attempt to foster and nurture multicultural understanding and awareness. The goal and challenge we set for ourselves was to give young people and the adults who serve them an opportunity to celebrate their own cultures and, at the very least, to gain an understanding of and perhaps a respect for cultures that are different from their own.

We decided that this forum should be an annual event. It would feature a writer, illustrator, publisher, or editor who had contributed significantly to cultural awareness. In order to attract and accommodate as large an audience as possible, this keynote presentation would be complemented by a number of workshops that would deal with specific cultural themes, issues, and topics presented from a variety of perspectives, namely, the artistic, literary, critical, educational, and developmental.

As we planned the format and content of the first conference, we hoped the event would motivate the participants to consider the types of questions we were addressing whenever we met:

> •What is the meaning of "culture" and how does the term apply to literature?

> •What images and messages does literature convey to children about the experiences of people who represent various cultural groups?

> •Which aspects of a culture—its values, beliefs, relationships, language, history, and traditions—are represented in literature for children and adolescents?

> •Can writers or illustrators ever present an accurate and authentic portrait of a culture that is not their own?

> •Can literature encourage young people to become sensitive to social and political issues that underpin every cultural group?

> •As Rudine Sims Bishop has suggested in the *Illinois English Bulletin*, is it possible for literature that depicts cultural experiences "to change us, to change our perspective on the world..."?

> • As professionals who work with children, what might we do to foster an understanding of cultural differences and similarities through literature and related arts?

At the time, it seemed that one promising sign was the fact that at our institution the building for gatherings of the sort we were planning is called the *Kiva*, the name given to the structure where Pueblo Indians hold their traditional ceremonies. In those early days of designing the Conference other invaluable encouragement came by way of the generous support of various constituencies within the Kent State University community and, outside of it, from the Cleveland Foundation and the George Gund Foundation.

NAMING THE CONFERENCE

It is not surprising that when it came to giving the conference a name we chose to honor Virginia Hamilton. An Ohio native, Virginia Hamilton is one of America's foremost writers for children and young adults. Born and raised in Yellow Springs, Ohio, where she now resides with her husband, award-winning poet Arnold Adoff, and their two children, Virginia Hamilton has received virtually every major award and honor accorded American authors of literature for youth. A member of the large Perry clan and the youngest child in her immediate family, she continues the Perry storytelling tradition through her work.

Since her first book *Zeely* appeared in 1967 and placed her at the forefront of contemporary juvenile writers, Ms. Hamilton has remained an inspiring writer of quality literature which speaks to readers of roots. She was the first African American to win the coveted Newbery Award for "the most distinguished contribution to literature for children," for *M. C. Higgins, the Great*, for which she also won the National Book Award and the Boston Globe Horn Book Award. Three other books, *The Planet of Junior Brown, Sweet Whispers, Brother Rush*, and *In the Beginning*, a collection of creation myths from around the world, have been named Newbery Honor books. In addition, Ms. Hamilton has twice been awarded a Certificate of Honor by the International Board on Books for Young People, and she has received the Coretta Scott King Award three times, most recently in 1986 for *The People Could Fly*, a collection of African American folktales. She is also the recipient of the 1988 Boston Globe Horn Book Award for *Anthony Burns*, a biography. Both *The Bells of Christmas*, a celebration of family life set in 1890s Ohio and *The Dark Way*, an international collection of mystery tales, have received wide critical acclaim. *Cousins*, a recent novel, was named a best book of 1990 by *Parenting* magazine. Among her many other honors, Ms. Hamilton has been selected to present the 1993 May Hill Arbuthnot Honor Lecture, and she is the winner of the 1992 Hans Christian Andersen Award.

Once Ms. Hamilton consented to having the conference bear her name, we invited her to inaugurate the event, on April 12, l985, by presenting the first keynote address. In this presentation, which she titled "The Spirit Spins: A Writer's Revolution," she discussed the traditions that have influenced her vision and traced her journey as a writer concerned with cultural authenticity.

At the first Virginia Hamilton Conference (called the Virginia Hamilton Lectureship on Minority Group Experiences in Children's Literature until l989), some 250 people, most of them from northeastern Ohio, chose to attend two of the six workshop offerings. Setting the precedent for the kinds of topics the Conference would continue to address in later years, the workshop leaders used lecture and demonstration to focus on both educational and literary issues that surround multiculturalism. For example, Mary Lou White, from Wright State University, discussed books that include characters from the southern Appalachians and ways to use these books in elementary and middle school classrooms, and Anita Moss, from the University of North Carolina, analyzed Virginia Hamilton's use of space as a metaphor for her characters' inner space, places where miraculous transformations and new possibilities may occur. The favorable assessment given the first Conference was summarized by one of the participants who wrote: "You have formed a touchstone event!"

EXPANDING THE CONFERENCE THEME

Since the inaugural Virginia Hamilton Conference of 1985, both the presenters and the participants have spurred us to move far beyond our original notion of culture. Motivated by their challenging questions and concerns, we have come to see how much we still need to know about this elusive and multifaceted concept called "culture." We have come to realize that there is no easy route to understanding a particular culture, that it is, in fact, just as valuable to consider the differences among us as it is to recognize the ties that bind us. In acknowledging and exploring both cultural differences and cultural similarities we somehow seem better positioned to discover and reflect on our mutual as well as distinct experiences, fears, dreams, and hopes.

By doing this, we can begin to sense what we don't yet know and understand about a culture different from our own, and we can admit to what we, as outsiders, may never be able to know or understand. Admitting these things, we are less likely to romanticize the life and habits of a cultural group and more likely to detect, examine, and counter the stereotypes and cliches that mask a group's true identity and keep the struggles and crises that characterize its history at a distance. Exploring children's literature from this perspective, we can gain new or different insights into the forces that shape a particular cultural group.

The ongoing dialogue generated by each of the presenters at the Virginia Hamilton Conference has brought us closer to understanding the nature and purpose of our responsibility to one another in this pluralistic world.

Since those early days of the Conference we have broadened what was once an exclusive concern for ethnicity and race to embrace what Virginia Hamilton calls "parallel cultures." What now drives the Conference is the need to look closely at the many different cultures that exist in tandem in a truly multicultural world. As the Conference has developed over its eight-year history, cross-culturalism has come to encompass many different aspects of culture, including gender, class and caste, regionalism, and the various social, political, and economic conditions that define a group's identity. The dimensions of multiculturalism espoused by the National Association of State Boards of Education in its recent publication, *The American Tapestry,* serve as the guide for what we hope to accomplish:

Education that is multicultural recognizes, accepts, values, affirms and promotes individual diversity in a pluralistic setting. Further, the term "multicultural" embraces and accepts the interdependence of many cultural groups within our country and the world at large: racial, ethnic, regional, religious, and socioeconomic groups, as well as men and women, the young and the old, and persons with disabilities.

MANY FACES, MANY VOICES

In *Many Faces, Many Voices*, the first volume of what promises to be a series of books on the Conference proceedings, we have selected both keynote and workshop presentations from several of the Conferences. Arnold Adoff sets the tone for this volume by inviting us to consider the social implications of the transformation that is occurring as our so-called minority population assumes its place as the majority. In "A Toiler, A Teller," Virginia Hamilton reflects on her life as an African American writer, as do Nicholasa Mohr and Sheila Hamanaka in a more political vein from their respective positions as an Hispanic American and Japanese American writer and artist. Both Ashley Bryan, in "Deep Like the Rivers," and Patricia and Fredrick McKissack, in an interview which captures the essence of their collaborative keynote presentation, reveal the forces that have shaped their sense of the cultures they depict in their award-winning books.

Representative of the workshop presentations that evoke so much rich dialogue at each of the Conferences there are Barbara Esbensen's illuminating demonstration of how she goes about retelling Ojibway tales; Gary Schmidt's appreciative examination of the ways in which writers such as Cynthia Rylant, Doris Buchanan Smith, and Gloria Houston present Appalachia as an almost Edenic region, despite the hardships that prevail there; Esther Cohen Hexter's comprehensive overview of a variety of books on the Jewish American experience, which takes us far beyond the customary concern for holidays; Arlene Mitchell's intriguing proposal for how to encourage young adults to "transact" with various types of multicultural literature by showing them that plot, for one example, is a series of vicarious life events which may feature new enterprise or inform the present; Darwin Henderson's suggestions for introducing young children to the rich and varied heritage of folk tales; and, finally, Marcella Anderson's first-hand account of the use of literature to help meet the emotional and cognitive needs of chronically ill children, a culture often overlooked.

The book concludes with three appendixes. The first appendix, "A Selected Listing of Multicultural Trade Books for Children and Young Adults," contains a variety of materials compiled by members of the Virginia Hamilton Conference Advisory Board. The second appendix, "Sources of Multicultural Materials," was compiled in response to the numerous requests from conference participants inquiring where to locate multicultural resources including books, educational programs, booklists, posters, realia and audiovisuals. The final, prepared by Alex Gilzden, Curator of Special Collections at Kent State University Library, describes the Virginia Hamilton Manuscript Collection. Ms. Hamilton has deposited many of her original manuscripts thus making it possible for scholars, teachers, and students of children's literature to study the development of her ideas.

ACKNOWLEDGMENTS

In more ways than we can mention, the Virginia Hamilton Conference is a collaborative event. Among the many people who have believed in the project from the start, we particularly have the following to thank for their continuing encouragement and generous support, without which the Conference would cease to exist:

The Advisory Board: Ione Cowen, Akron-Summit County Library; Julie Gedeon, Kent State University School of Library and Information Science; Darwin Henderson, Purdue University; Nora Kegley, Kent, Ohio; Bonnie Kelly, Kent State University; Yvette Kirksey, Akron City Schools; Dan MacLachlan, Akron City Schools; Mercier

Robinson, East Cleveland Public Library; Jan Smuda, Project LEAP, Cuyahoga County Public Library; Dave Tirpak, Orange City Schools; and Jan Wojnaroski, Kent City Schools.

For their continuing funding assistance: Priscilla Drach, Cuyahoga County Public Library; Steven Hawk, Akron-Summit County Public Library; and Irwin Dinn, the Victor C. Laughlin, M. D., Memorial Foundation Trust.

For help in establishing the Conference: The Cleveland Foundation; the George Gund Foundation; Sue Misheff, Malone College; at Kent State University: Leo Anglin, Associate Dean, College of Education; Robert Bamberg, Department of English; Edward and Shirley Crosby, Pan African Studies Program; Eugene Wenninger and Carol Toncar, Research and Sponsored Programs; Nora Kegley, former Coordinator, College of Continuing Studies; Charles F. Kegley, Chair, Adult, Counseling, Health, and Vocational Education; Don L. Tolliver, Dean of Library and Media Services; Mary K. Biagini, former Acting Dean, School of Library and Information Science; and the late A. R. Rogers, Dean, School of Library and Information Science.

Kent State University: Dean Rosemary Ruhig Du Mont, School of Library and Information Science; Dean Joanne Rand Whitmore, College of Education; Dean Marlene Dorsey, College of Continuing Studies; JoAnne L. Vacca, Chair, Department of Teacher Development and Curriculum Studies; the staff of the College of Continuing Studies, especially Lori Gourley, Program Coordinator, Geri Ash, Gretchen Laflin, Su Tams, and Carolyn Boykin; Alex Gilzden, Curator, Special Collections, University Library; John Brett Buchanan, Creative Director, GLYPHIX; Kathleen Willey, University Foundation; Vicky Quintos, School of Art; and the many graduate and undergraduate students who have helped manage each Conference.

Highsmith Press for inviting us to reach a wider audience, especially Donald J. Sager, Publisher, and Nancy Wilcox, Managing Editor.

Janet Loch for her patient editorial assistance.

And, of course, many thanks to all the many presenters.

Anthony L. Manna
Carolyn S. Brodie

Illustration by Symeon Shimin. From *Zeely* by Virginia Hamilton. Copyright
© 1967 by Macmillan Publishing Company. Reprinted with the permission of the
publisher.

1

A TOILER, A TELLER

BY VIRGINIA HAMILTON

I am a "toiler of 'tells'" or a "teller of toils," a tunesmith of language and mind-talk for the young-and-breathless and their older handlers. I am one part story-bold and another part perpetually twelve. Thus, I will keep forever marvelous memories from my childhood, some having to do with my relatives out-doing one another by their wit with words.

Having been born in one of our bleaker states, Ohio, I suspect I evolved into a scribbler out of the desperate desire to create a less melancholy, dryer clime. Ohio has some of the hardest rains, the gentlest, sweetest fogs, and some of the richest soil in the country, which is the reason a "toilsome of laborers" such as my relatives are beholden to this verdant land. However, the state is also known for its harrowing droughts, which I have portrayed in a new book titled *Drylongso*. But I am descended from black-dirt farmers who faired well through thick and thin, (and one odd musician, my dad, who I'll speak about later,) eccentric individuals who never failed to see the humor in an Ohio landscape, wet or dry.

Here's how a bit of it goes:

Uncle L. E. saying that God had seen Ohio but three times. The first time was when He created it. The second time was when He returned to apologize for what He'd done. The last time (which was last week or the last frost, depending on the whim of the uncle or aunt disguised as a follower of the plow who is telling the tale) when

God came to play the Ohio Lotto and lost His new bib overalls. "Got them on sale at Sears, don't you know."

Uncle L. E. saying, if God had-a won the lottery, he'dve had the means and the leisure to move Lake Erie down from the upper tier so poor Cousin Lucrecia and Cousin Jason up at Cleveland would get a rest from the confound winter winds coming in off that blasted Lake...

The above two paragraphs being a rambling section of a tall tale, known as a God Tale in my family, and added to over generations. I remember hearing such tales when I was ten or eleven, mainly from my uncles. Uncles didn't have much to say to children, often; I suppose they were too busy farming. At any rate, they didn't talk in the manner of mothers and aunts.

"She's getting tall," aunts always did say. Or, "Sit up straight," said our mothers. "Take that rouge off your face. Acting just like Cousin Lolly Dee, and you know what happened to *her*."

No, we didn't know what happened to Cousin Lolly Dee. But aunts and mothers knew they had us close by them all day, waiting eagerly to hear *the rest of the story*.

My childhood was never as crystalline as I make it out to be. But it was good in ways that remain important to me. Around my youth was abundant space and time. There was never the clutter of too much activity or motion for its own sake. There was no hurry to go somewhere or to do some organized playing every minute. I remember well that there was time for my cousins and myself to be utterly bored. We grew so tired of fields, dusty roads, the tedium of clotheslines, of feeding chickens, sweating in the heat, staring at flies, with the excruciating dullness of country sameness day upon day, that we would imagine anything, and we made up whopping lies about everything we could think of. We spent hours at my cousin's house swinging on the porch swing, thinking up things to do. An entire day might go by with us holed up in the shade, conjuring a special something that would be worth the supreme effort of getting up off our skinny behinds. I recall that one time, we did have quite a thought.

One of us thought up the bright idea of walking the three-inch wide oak cross-beam 30 feet up almost to the top of Uncle Willy's hay barn. We then had a serious discussion about the proper method of crossing the beam. Finally, we decided that the best way to get from one side to the other without falling would be to walk barefoot. But then we thought that the most exciting way would be to go barefoot while running across. And the most daring—the most scary—way would have to be barefoot, running and *blindfolded*. Well, it would necessarily be a slow, cautious run. The blindfolds stayed *on*; and we accomplished all three ways.

I told this true tale to my daughter and received a withering look of disdain, followed by, "Dumb...country...Didn't you guys know you could've been killed?"

No, I don't think any of us ever believed that we could have even fallen. Not because we hadn't the sense to realize. But because we were by then terribly skilled at being kids. We didn't cross the high beam out of folly. I think we chose the beam because it was a challenge for us, to our abilities.

In the same fashion. M. C. Higgins (from *M. C. Higgins, the Great*) chose to sit on his pole, swim the Ohio River; Buddy Clark (from *The Planet of Junior Brown*) chose to live on his own, overseeing his planets of homeless kids; Arilla (from *Arilla Sun Down*) chose to secretly go out at night roller skating; Justice (from *Justice and Her Brothers*) would mind-jump to a distant future; and Cammy (from *Cousins*) sneaked into a nursing home in broad daylight to visit her grandmother. Such visits were forbidden a child her age unaccompanied by an adult.

My cousins and I were as agile as cats, risk-takers, just like the characters from my novels. We were in excellent physical shape since we traveled everywhere by means of

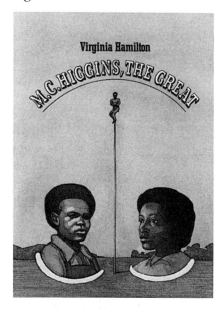

Jacket illustration by James McMullan. From *M. C. Higgins, the Great* by Virginia Hamilton. Copyright © 1974 by Macmillan Publishing Company. Reprinted with the permission of the publisher.

3

our own locomotion. We were expert at fence walking, rope jumping, bike acrobatics (shades of *Justice* again), and sleeping out at night on the slanted tin roof of the chicken coop without once sliding off or waking up from dreams (hints of this in *Zeely*). Barehanded, we subdued fighting tomcats; we buried beloved pets crushed by automobiles. We learned the piney woods, (woods scenes in *Willie Bea and the Time the Martians Landed*, *A Little Love* and *Arilla Sun Down*) how to catch fly balls, how to turn back a pack of wild dogs—the shrillness of our terrified yells and the accuracy of thrown stones worked every time. Rarely did we call our parents when we were in trouble; but rather, we depended on the skill and courage of one another. My cousins and I were survivors. And the danger of the highbeam in Uncle Willy's hay barn was for us made considerably less, yet was terribly significant to our growth. This true tale can be found threaded neatly through the fiction of *Willie Bea and the Time the Martians Landed*.

Without such vivid recollections such as the highbeam walk, several of my books may not have been written, at least, would not have had so rich a tapestry.

Having experienced Ohio drought, I wrote *Drylongso* with a steady hand. Having a grandfather who was a fugitive from slavery gave me personal, emotional insight into an ethnic, racial tragedy. From there I was able to compose *Anthony Burns: The Defeat and Triumph of a Fugitive Slave*; *The People Could Fly: American Black Folk Tales* and its companion volume out in the winter of 1993, *Many Thousand Gone: African Americans from Slavery to Freedom*. All three books are what I term Liberation Literature. Through reading about the suffering and tribulations of others, we bear witness, our spirits fly free, we are liberated, as were so many thousands gone before us.

I connect with time present and time past through story telling, using also my knowledge of historical fact. My father was a tale-teller and a classical mandolinist who played in mandolin clubs across this country (he died at the age of 80 in 1960). For many years he made his living in such musical groups, which by

4

the way, were integrated in the early 1900s not only black and white but male and female as well (I have the old photographs). Dad was an artist, a loner and a wanderer, a man of mild mood swings and long silences. In later years, he wandered well back in his mind and consistently brought up good stories. Sitting there in the firelight and safety of our home place, he taught me how a story began and how it ended through the steady, sonorous tones of his Midwestern voice.

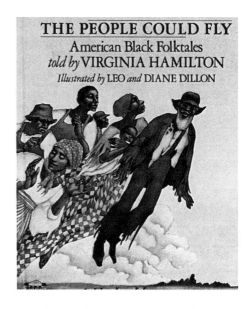

From *The People Could Fly: American Black Folktales*, told by Virginia Hamilton and illustrated by Leo and Diane Dillon. Reprinted by permission of Alfred A. Knopf, Inc.

Dad would begin, "Did I ever tell you about the time...I discovered this bear hunter in Calgary, Alberta, Canada?"

"No!" I said, "Was he lost?"

"I am still undecided about that," he said, "But I found the bear he was after before he did!" And off he'd go with the story, perhaps too long to tell here. I'll save it for you for some other time!

Mother, on the other hand, would start a story with—I remember something about that...let's see...Reminds me of the time all of the ivy fell from Mrs. Pinton's house."

"All of it? All at once—when did that happen?" I asked. And mother was off and running with the tale about "the day the ivy fell." It can be found in its entirety, part true, part fiction or fancy, part tragic, in my novel *Sweet Whispers, Brother Rush*.

I learned from my parents' telling that accounting, or narrating made me feel better. Moreover, writing one word down after another in narration, in accounts of events, marked the passage of time. Words in progression across the page take us where we want to go without placing our fragile beings in jeopardy. I create and recreate my own experiences, who I am, through memory and imagination formed into a creative writing process. My thoughts and ideas are translated at once into characters. Characters redefine the artistic self and recreate it. Created characters are my way of reaching out from inside myself to the reader and what we hold in common among us. That must be our sensibility and our humanity.

Writing from an inside place, I have a strong need to go out and know and be known by the community, village, and world. I write from a parallel American culture of African Americans, which culture was at one time in the past, in the Plantation Era, wholly outside the American mainstream. Presently, it weaves strongly in and out of other group cultures. Parallel culture best describes the polyethnic, culturally diverse communities of present-day America.

I've attempted to mark the history and traditions of one parallel culture people, African Americans, through my writings, while bringing readers strong stories and memorable characters living their lives the best they know how. My purpose as a novelist, biographer, and creator and compiler of stories has been to entertain, to write well through the story lines, and to introduce readers to the joys of literate language.

Unfortunately, the young people who most need to read books like mine may never read them. They are never still enough, focused enough, nor do they have a calm environment in which to read. Many may not know how to read. How can there be readers when the young lack the safe environment where reading can take place? One comes to realize that reading and writing are leisure, often elite occupations. But we continue forward, trying to capture those young people who can be taken by story.

I remain strong in the belief that the imaginative use of language and ideas can illuminate a human condition. It is my hope that readers, the child and the adult, will learn to care about who the characters are, that they will come to feel and understand them, and empathize with them. Perhaps they will come to see that characters are ourselves, real people in disguise.

I see myself as a skater gliding back and forth, to and fro, from many allegiances—to sisterhood, motherhood, wife, to country, to ethnic group, to family, and to mother earth. There is a common bond among us, writer and reader, that we are not without the other. Writers connect with and in. We cannot do without. Ours is a multicultural, polycentric, pluralistic nation of the world village where we must enter into the bond of learning and understanding together, in community.

A SELECTED LISTING OF BOOKS BY VIRGINIA HAMILTON

All Jahdu Storybook. San Diego, CA: Harcourt, Brace & Jovanovich, 1991.

Anthony Burns: The Defeat and Triumph of a Fugitive Slave. New York: Knopf, 1988.

Arilla Sun Down. New York: Greenwillow, 1976.

The Bells of Christmas. Illustrated by Lambert Davis. San Diego, CA: Harcourt, Brace & Jovanovich, 1989.

Cousins. New York: Putnam, 1990.

The Dark Way: Stories from the Spirit World. Illustrated by Lambert Davis. San Diego, CA: Harcourt, Brace & Jovanovich, 1990.

Drylongso. Illustrated by Jerry Pinkney. San Diego, CA: Harcourt, Brace & Jovanovich, 1992.

Dustland. New York: Greenwillow, 1980.

The Gathering. New York: Greenwillow, 1981.

The House of Dies Drear. Illustrated by Eros Keith. New York: Macmillan, 1968.

In the Beginning: Creation Stories from Around the World. Illustrated by Barry Moser. San Diego, CA: Harcourt, Brace & Jovanovich, 1988.

Jahdu. Illustrated by Jerry Pinkney. New York: Greenwillow, 1980.

Junius Over Far. New York: Harper Junior Books, 1985.

Justice and Her Brothers. New York: Greenwillow, 1978.

A Little Love. New York: Putnam, 1984.

M. C. Higgins, the Great. New York: Macmillan, 1974.

The Magical Adventures of Pretty Pearl. New York: Harper Junior Books, 1983.

The Mystery of Drear House: The Conclusion of the Dies Drear Chronicle. New York: Greenwillow, 1987.

Paul Robeson: The Life and Times of a Free Black Man. New York: Harper Junior Books, 1974.

The People Could Fly: American Black Folktales. Illustrated by Leo and Diane Dillon. New York: Knopf, 1986.

The Planet of Junior Brown. New York: Macmillan, 1971.

Sweet Whispers, Brother Rush. New York: Putnam, 1982.

Time-Ago Lost! More Tales of Jahdu. Illustrated by Ray Ranther. New York: Macmillan, 1973.

W. E. B. DuBois: A Biography. New York: Crowell, 1972.

A White Romance. New York: Putnam, 1987.

Willie Bea and the Time the Martians Landed. New York: Greenwillow, 1983.

Zeely. Illustrated by Symeon Shimin. New York: Macmillan, 1967.

THE NEXT AMERICA

BY ARNOLD ADOFF

My Fellow Americans:

I Am Travelling Around This Chaos Country Talking About:
The Next Step, The Next Dance, the Next America: Trying
To Point Our Chins Up Over The Garbage-Pile Sightlines And
Horror Horizons Of T h e s e T i m e s. I Speak Speeches.
I Read Poems. I Organize Panels Of "Parallel Culture" Writers
And Artists: Side-By-Side Visions Of Our Immediate Futures.
It Is Always A Struggle, This Wealth And Hunger Synthesis
Called "The Land Of The Free." And For An Aging Poet, Raised
Under Flags Of Past Revolutions, That Word "Struggle"
Should Be Enough To Define Self-Image. We Can Talk
About The Rest Next May, In Kent, Ohio. Perhaps:
We Shall Stroll The Campus, Unafraid,
W h i s p e r i n g F u t u r e s
W i t h o u t
          R o e
             V .
     W a d e .

Now: Read This Poem.
    Read It For The Fantasy/Reality "Story"
    Of A F r o z e n M o m e n t On Broadway
    In My Beloved New York City.
Then: Close Your Eyes. Did Your Grandmother Take The Subway
    In The Dark Mornings, Seventy Years Ago, Her Sewing
    Machine On Her Back: Strapped Down For The D a i l y
    J o u r n e y To The Damned (And Daily Bread) Shop?
    (And if her back was covered by a sack of just-picked cotton,
    or a bunch of branches, or a fine silk shawl: then just
    magnify the richness of our future campus conversations. . . .)
Then: Open Your Eyes.
    Read This Poem Again.
Now: Take A Deep Breath And Step Outside.

Journal Entry: Daily Flight Down Broadway

I Fly Down From The 37th Floor. Land Soft On Sidewalk. My Long
Warm Coat Trails Behind.   Jet Plane Vapor Trail Of Apartment
And Order. The Dishes Are Washed And Put Away Neat. Leftovers
Under Plastic. In Full Refrigerator. Daily Flight Down Broadway.

Act Two.
Act Too.
The Story So Far.
The Woman Is Sitting On A Piece Of Cardboard. In The Doorway
Next To The Cash Machine Of The Chemical Bank. She Smiles.
Her Daughter Smiles And Eats Cut Pieces Of Fresh Fruit.

Plastice Garbage Bags. Shopping Cart. Crutches. Wheelchairs Rising
To The Skies. Dogs Patrolling The Gates Of Hell.   Full
                                                    Chorus
                        Of Angels Singing
                                   Back
                                   Up.

There Is Change In The Coffee Cup
At The Feet Of The Woman. Mother.
Nobody Wants To Talk. Who TheHell
Would Want To Tell You A Story
                              In The Cold Afternoon
                              In The Doorway Next
                                            To
                              The Cash Machine?

I Need To Know If The Girl Is Going To School Each Day.
I Need To Know Where They Sleep Each Night.
I Need To Know If the Girl Has Organized Her Notebook Into Subjects.
Is There A Shelter Safe Shelter For The Night?
Does The Girl Have A Full Supply Of Sharpened NumberTwoPencils?
Do I Need To Know Preferred Brand Of Deodorant?
Do I Need To Know Preferred Brand Of Cereal?
Breakfast   Of   Doorways.
Coffee
Break   Of   Doorways.
Afternoons Of   Doorways.

I Am Filming This Commercial With My Eyes. My Mouth Is Empty
And Dry. My Lips Are Shut Tight Even As I Smile At The girl
And Her Mother And Put Some Of My Money Into Their Cup.
I Keep My Questions And Words   Behind My Eyes . And Walk.
Broadway.
The Streets Are Paved With Gold.
The Ghost Of My Sweet Grandmother Glides Down From The Roof
Of The Metropolitan Opera House And Over The Old Cobblestones.
The Old Sewing Machine Is Still On Her Back. Some Eternal Hump
Under The Long White Robe.
The Wind From Her   Wings
                                        Lifts
Me Over   The Chemical Bank
Building And Over   The Met
To Some Celestial   CoffeeShop
Where We Both Order Prune
                          Danish
                          And
                          Hot Tea.

I   Can   Hear   T h a n k Y o u Rising From The Street
                                        Like A Curse On My Soul.[1]

NOTES

1. Adoff, Arnold. "The Next America," © Copyright 1992. This piece is from a collection he is editing for future publication called "The Next America."

ABOUT THE AUTHOR

As a poet and anthologist, Arnold Adoff has published more than 30 books for young readers and their "older allies." His work includes *Black is Brown is Tan*, *All the Colors of the Race*, *I Am the Running Girl*, *Sports Pages*, *Eats: Poems, Chocolate Dreams*, and recently, *In for Winter, Out for Spring*, illustrated by Jerry Pinkney. He studied American history at City College of the City University of New York and at Columbia University and writing at the New School in New York City. He was a teacher and counselor in the New York City public schools for 12 years. Mr. Adoff received the 1988 Award for Excellence in Poetry given by the National Council of Teachers of English. He was Distinguished Visiting Professor at the School of Education of Queens College of the City University. He is married to noted author Virginia Hamilton, and they divide their time between New York City and Yellow Springs, Ohio.

2

THE MAGIC OF IMAGINING TRANSACTION WITH YOUNG ADULT FICTION AND POETRY

BY ARLENE HARRIS MITCHELL

Jerry was a good student. She was quiet, worked appropriately, answered when she was called on, was always courteous. But she didn't like to read. She read the assignments and did the required work, but she wasn't touched or engaged in the books. As part of my personal objective to make the classroom more student centered, I decided that Jerry was a good study. Could I get her interested in reading? As part of my quest, I allowed students to self-select books for their personal enjoyment. Even this didn't work for Jerry. Here was an eighth grade student who found reading a chore. I stepped in and suggested three books to her. Being a conscientious student, she felt compelled to accept one and chose Sharon Bell Mathis' *Teacup Full of Roses*. After reading the book, and responding to it in her own way (adding a dialog between Joy, Davey, and Paul), she read the other two suggested books, Mildred Taylor's *The Road to Memphis*, and Virginia Hamilton's *M. C. Higgins, the Great*. She became so enthused with these offerings and her own reactions to them, that she suggested *Listen for the Fig Tree* to the teacher.

Many of us who are involved in the world of literature, English teachers and librarians especially, often wonder what happens to students after grade five that they begin to lose the wonderful gift for imagining through their reading and writing. They become hearers not listeners, reporters not writers, and clones not creators.

As educators, we need to investigate what we have done that limits that wonderful world of imagination.

Part of the fault lies in the "curriculum" that most secondary schools have put into place. A curriculum that relies on a highly traditional, highly canonized, highly boring assortment of works—which gives little or no time for appreciation or enjoyment of learning. What I have found during 21 years of teaching, however, is that the curriculum seldom, if ever, dictates what one *can't* do in the curriculum. And it is upon that premise that I share the following scenarios.

Students need an opportunity to transact with literature. It is not enough to read *required* pieces and to answer pre-packaged questions with preordained answers, put in place by someone who may understand literature but who has never met our students. Yet this is the way many literature curricula work. The textbook is not a resource for accomplishing the objectives of the course. Instead, the textbook *is* the objective of the course — sometimes an unreasonable amount of material. Teachers begin to cover the text, covering the curriculum while students are left behind trying to deal with the C on the last test, knowing that the next test can't be much better, and wondering "What is the right answer?" This special emphasis on "cover" is to maintain that to "cover" the material is not to teach it and not to learn it. It is to gloss over and turn pages, hoping that bits and pieces will be retained in the learners' minds in the process.

We need to realize that our students bring a wealth of knowledge to the classroom. They did not begin to learn when they came into our seventh, ninth or twelfth grade class—or even when they appeared at our kindergarten doors. They bring to schools five, ten, fifteen years, of knowledge, of experiences.

Unfortunately, not all of the school-based knowledge gathering has been as challenging as it might have been, and certainly not as creative as it appeared in the earlier grades. It has been question-response and multiple choice, all with predetermined answers on which the student has learned she or he either does well or fails. When we get a student in seventh or tenth grade who has had years of experience of failure, of feeling that what he or she knows is of no value unless it contains the "right" answer, we are beginning at a disadvantage—both teacher and student. As educators, we need to begin valuing the voice of our students. Louise Rosenblatt (1983) stated that

> Instead of judgements accepted in whole cloth [the learner] must acquire a curiosity about the causes of human actions and social conditions; he must be ready to revise accepted hypothesis in light of new information. . . . He needs, in short, to develop a dynamic sense of life. . . .[1] When a student has been moved by a work of literature, he will be led to ponder on questions of right or wrong, of admirable or antisocial qualities, of justifiable or unjustifiable actions.[2]

To begin to accept any part of this theory, we must begin by giving a variety of experiences that will pique this curiosity and offer various opportunities for the student to pose questions, explore for answers, and revise or affirm their reactions. Learning activities will vary depending on what the student brings to the environment and the stimulus that the teacher or others have provided. When all that we provide are textbooks and pre-prepared questions and answers, students know that their ideas are not valued, and that we really do not intend for them to explore the literature and find their own aesthetic, social, and intellectual values.

Most of us who are literature teachers or librarians have come to these roles because of our love for literature. We know that we learn about our world and our society from literature. We gain aesthetic appreciation through our reading of literature. We know that there is an element of "self" as we read. We find pieces that are new and rewarding over and over as we read and teach. We respond to the poem or story with personal engagement—not preconceived interpretations. Yet, we expect our students to accept an interpretation that has been argued among scholars, or to find for themselves the *accepted* interpretation. Let's challenge students to use their imagination and to explore to make meaning.

Many educators are aware of the importance of expanding the creative activities and the critical thinking of their students as part of their literature program. For some reason, however, we tend not to follow through with these important issues in the name of time and curriculum. What we need to remember is that we teach young adults, not curriculum. We want life-long learners and creative thinkers. When we infuse the value of person and defuse the importance of text, when we infuse the value of exploring ideas and defuse the need for one correct answer; we begin to see the real value of a range of literature, a range of responses, a range of interest, and a range of possibilities. Some strategies which facilitate students' thinking and imagination are quite simple yet satisfy the hidden agenda of exploration desired by most teachers. Let's make this an open agenda and an integral part of our classes.

1. *Introduce literature as a fun activity—not a chore of the curriculum.* Use personalized reactions and journal writings to explore the aesthetics and the purpose of the literature. During a recent workshop activity, the following student responses were shared.

> The first poem ("To Jesus Villanueva") was written in a very untraditional form that's not even free verse. It doesn't . . . . I can't express it. I don't quite understand it, but I'd love to have you show me. I like it, and I know it has a great deal of meaning all the same.

> A lot of flow to it, a lot of rhythm.

> I was just going to say about the same poem, it gives a good mood. . . reminds me of a letter from a relative.

> I liked "Each Morning." It's got personification in it. I felt he was searching for something he never had. . . the sunrise or whatever; did he really remember his father with love. It seems he's looking for a father where there was none.

> I just felt it was visual. I liked the sea; it was very visual. I felt I could paint it, and it had a sad feeling to it.

> But I felt the last sentence is ironic sounding, almost as though he could be laughing.

These various comments were made after reading three different poems: "Each Morning" by Imamu Amiri Baraka; "To Jesus Villanueva, with Love" by Alma Villanueva; and "My Brother Estes" by Jo Carson. The participants were responding to a very simple reaction prompt, "Give your first reaction or feelings about any one of the poems we have read"; and in their own language, they began to talk about imagery, figurative language and interpretation. More important, however, they began to share across the poems, interjecting comments that made other students *want* to revisit the poems they had not written about. We now had a starting base that *they* had established.

2. *Integrate the genres.* The study of one genre for long periods of time becomes boring to both teacher and students. A thematic approach allows for the integration across genres and the addition of other content areas as well as art and music supplements. To do this well, teachers must know as much about literature as they can. This means reading, reading, reading, and listening to what students say about what they read and what they like to read. It means that in addition to reading the traditional, anthologized, and canonized works, we must read young adult literature, literature across all cultures, literature across genre, and across content areas.

We must begin to disclaim the notion that every student must read the same book, or the same story or the same poem always at the same time, for the same purpose. When we do this, we limit the range of ideas that students bring to the text. By using stories from Paula Gunn Allen's *The Woman Who Owned the Shadows*, poems from Nikki Giovanni's *The Women and the Men*, and Toshio Mori's stories from *Yokohama, California*, students could respond from a variety of readings in relationship to a few selected topics such as characterization, tone, language. These could be used in conjunction with selected works from the anthology or other curriculum lists, if they are required. Students will begin to see that language changes as appropriate for the type of story and the purpose of the writer—just as language changes for them as they communicate among themselves in informal settings, with adults, in school, and in the play areas. They begin to see the similarities and differences among cultures (Native American, African American and Japanese American) and how the experiences of these diverse relationships help students to define themselves.

The greatest value may be that they investigate not one story or one idea, but a variety of stories and experiences. They will begin to value libraries, knowing that real books exist for purposes beyond the established anthology. Many students look upon the anthology and the required books of the classroom as the only important reading in existence. If they do not enjoy this literature, they begin to question the aesthetics and purpose of all literature. This strategy works exceptionally well in classes which have a range of learning abilities or interests. Without feeling intimidated or misplaced, students begin to investigate for themselves, finding a world of literary offerings that they did not know existed.

3. *Read with the students, read to the students, let students read to each other.* The enjoyment of listening to a story does not stop after grade four. Senior high students enjoy listening to a well-read, interesting or fun piece of literature. So often, the excited voice that the teacher gives to a work invites the students to read the work. To encourage students to choose a work or a passage to share with the class is to encourage students to make the oral reading interesting. This type of reading is much different from the mundane, monotones that we get when students take turns reading aloud from a text—often without any opportunity to pre-read the passage. It takes practice but many students who have been labeled or who have had failings in the world of reading, have found that they can be promising orators when they choose a work of interest to them and practice it for others to hear. I still remember the passionate reading of a tenth grader from the *Year of Impossible Goodbyes* by Sook Nyul Choi. As Sookan and her younger brother Inchun hid in the corn fields during their escape to South Korea, Donald read to the class in a whispered voice,

The dark cornfield up ahead seemed to be harboring all sorts of evil creatures and I imagined them whispering, "Go back to the old man and stay with him. You won't make it through here." I looked at the package I was clutching, opened it, and gave a rice cake to Inchun. He ate in silence and I know he was swallowing his tears as he ate. . . Inchun sat quietly and then exclaimed, "Look, look over there! It's like a rainbow. Look how it moves." He pointed to the left side of the field and then to the right. I saw a bright greenish-colored beam covering the ground.[3]

We listened to Donald carefully and the pride he felt from his attentive audience was visible. One of the students asked why he had chosen that particular selection, and he responded, "I like the description of train and how the conductor helped them. And I like the way the search light looked like a rainbow." When another student asked what happened at the end, Donald beamed and said, "You have to read the book." Then he promised to tell the story to the student, but privately, so that it wasn't ruined for the other students. Students need to understand that they bring meaning to the text. These are only words on a paper until the reader makes them come alive.

4. *Let students contract for grades, for selections, for completion.* This allows students to accept some responsibility for the learning and gives them an opportunity to express their learning when they have accomplished the objective. It also extends the value of the portfolio, allowing students to select and complete works and assignments as they make them ready for public review.

When Jerry suggested to me that *Listen for the Fig Tree* had been a special book for her, she was completing and upgrading a contract. By providing varied opportunities for students to explore the literature, they are encouraged and have time to grow into the feel of the works. Jerry had tried several books before I suggested *Teacup Full of Roses*. But with the contract, she had time to catch up and to make her B an A for the project. Meanwhile, she was a participant in the discussions, even if not a happy one.

When we read, "The Reason I Like Chocolates," another student discovered Nikki Giovanni with the same fervor that Jerry discovered Sharon Bell Mathis. And although this poem was not in the anthology, the smiles it brought to the faces of the students as they read and reread, responding in writing of their own "The reason I like. . ." was much more creative and involved more critical thinking than any dissection of a Shakespearean sonnet would have accomplished. What they later learned, in fact, was that Shakespeare, too, could be understood when approached in this way.

5. *Give opportunities for students to respond in a variety of ways— writing, demonstrations, illustrations, musical selections.* Children are naturally creative and inquisitive—simply not all in the same direction or taking on the same characteristics. Not all students have a talent for schooling as it is generally presented. If we provide opportunities for students to respond in a variety of ways, however, we tap that creative talent.

Some students enjoy writing and write well. Other students have problems writing and do not communicate well in this form. They have the ideas, but fall short in the written communication. We need to nurture this talent for each type of student. The student who enjoys writing or who writes well generally succeeds in school because that is the way they are most often asked to communicate their knowledge. But some students are creative with their hands; they draw and carve; they build and fix. Some students are creative in music. They sing or play instruments or dance. They compose and improvise.

6. *Give students opportunities to think through their ideas in responding to literature, to share those ideas and to alter or reaffirm their thinking.* A classroom environment that welcomes transaction is one that states through teacher and setting that diversity in interests, personalities, talents, and imagination are welcome here. But make no mistake, it also states that there is a "work" ethic. Learning is hard work. But concern, encouragement, and love of learning are also openly generated.

During a curriculum workshop, I worked with teachers to develop a unit which included decision making and its consequences. Passages from Walter Dean Myers' *Fallen Angels* elicited relevant and profound personal reactions from the very beginning:

> "Hey Perry!"
> "What did you do back in the World?"
> "Just got out of school," I said.
> "You didn't finish either?"
> "I finished high school."
> "Then why you come in the army?"
> "Seemed like a good idea at the time."[4]

Students began questioning whether or not people should join the army, the place for females, the options after school. Those who continued to read the book, wrote about reality versus dreams, what they are told to believe compared to how they should see things for themselves. While reading *I Know Why the Caged Bird Sings*, another option during this unit, students became acquainted with Maya Angelou's poetry as well. Her collection *Shaker, Why Don't You Sing?* is appropriate for most high school students, and it gives students an opportunity to hear another voice from the same author.

Use the library or media center as a major source for finding a wealth of literature—not just for research. The librarian or media specialist welcomes the opportunity to share their knowledge of the holdings. As you can see from the examples here, the possibilities are not limited to young adult literature, but include literature written for elementary children. This is an important aspect because older children will miss out on the new literature by Pat McKissack, Laurence Yep, John Steptoe, and others just because they were born too early to be invited into the world of these wonderful children's books. One way to incorporate these books is thematically. For example, Virginia Hamilton's *In the Beginning* is a wonderful source when doing mythology, creation stories, or other themes. Faith Ringgold's story *Tar Beach* is creatively told and colorfully illustrated with beautiful "patch" drawings. Nancy Wood's *Many Winters* is a wonderful book of Native American's feelings

NATIVE AMERICAN
STORIES *Told by Joseph Bruchac*

From KEEPERS OF THE EARTH
Michael J. Caduto and Joseph Bruchac
Foreword by N. Scott Momaday
Illustrations by John Kahionhes Fadden

Illustration by John Kahiohes Fadden. From *Native American Stories Told by Joseph Bruchac*. Copyright © 1991 by Joseph Bruchac. Reprinted with permission.

about their world, and the drawings and paintings by Frank Howell are fascinating. Kazue Mizumura's book of haiku *Flower Moon Snow* is also interesting, easy, and fun. Other good sources of variety for stories and poems include Caduto and Bruchac's *Native American Stories Told by Joseph Bruchac*, Faderman and Bradshaw's *Speaking for Ourselves*, Katharine Newmans's *Ethnic American Short Stories*, and Marilyn Smith Layton's *Intercultural Journeys Through Reading and Writing* to name a few.

Encourage students to use their imagination. Let them know that they as learners, their ideas, and reactions are valued. More importantly, as a teacher, believe it. Celebrate the learning.

NOTES

1. Rosenblatt, *Literature as Exploration*, 132.

2. Ibid., 17.

3. Nyul Choi, *Year of Impossible Goodbyes*, 158-59.

4. Myers, *Fallen Angels*, 13.

WORKS CITED

Allen, Paula Gunn. *The Woman Who Owned the Shadows*. San Francisco: Spinsters/Aunt Lute, 1983.

Angelou, Maya. *I Know Why the Caged Bird Sings*. New York: Bantam Books, 1973.

———. *Shaker, Why Don't You Sing?* New York: Random House, 1983.

Baraka, Imamu Amirai. *Preface to a Twenty Volume Suicide Note*. New York: Totem Corinth Books, 1961.

Caduto, Michael J. and Bruchac, Joseph. *Native American Stories told by Joseph Bruchac*. Golden, CO: Fulcrum Publishing, 1991.

Carson, Jo. *Stories I Ain't Told Nobody Yet*. New York: Orchard Books, 1989.

Choi Sook Nyul. *Year of Impossible Goodbyes*. Boston: Houghton Mifflin, 1991.

Faderman, Lillian and Bradshaw, Barbara. *Speaking for Ourselves*. Glenview, IL: Scott, Foresman, 1969.

Giovanni, Nikki. *The Women and the Men*. New York: William Morrow, 1975.

Hamilton, Virginia. *In the Beginning: Creation Stories from Around the World*. San Diego: Harcourt Brace Jovanovich, 1988.

———. *M.C. Higgins, the Great*. New York: Macmillan, 1974.

Layton, Marilyn Smith. *Intercultural Journeys Through Reading and Writing*. New York: Harper Collins, 1991.

Mathis, Sharon Bell. *Listen for the Fig Tree*. New York: Puffin Books, 1990.

———. *Teacup Full of Roses*. New York: Puffin Books, 1987.

Mizumura, Kazue. *Flower Moon Snow: A Book of Haiku*. New York: Thomas Y. Crowell, 1977.

Mori, Toshio. *Yokohama, California*. Seattle: University of Washington Press, 1985.

Myers, Walter Dean. *Fallen Angels*. New York: Scholastic, 1988.

Newman, Katharine, Ed. *Ethnic American Short Stories*. Boston: Allyn and Bacon, 1975.

Ringgold, Faith. *Tar Beach*. New York: Crown Publishers, 1991.

Rosenblatt, Louise. *Literature as Exploration*, 4th ed. New York: Modern Language Association of American, 1983.

Taylor, Mildred D. *The Road to Memphis*. New York: Dial Books, 1990.

Villanueva, Alma. "To Jesus Villanueva, with Love." In *Contemporary Chicano Poetry: A Critical Approach to an Emerging Literature*, Marta Ester Sanchez, Ed. Los Angeles: University of California Press, 1985.

Wood, Nancy. *Many Winters: Prose and Poetry of the Pueblos*. Garden City, NY: Doubleday, 1974.

ABOUT THE AUTHOR

Arlene Harris Mitchell received her Ph.D. from The Pennsylvania State University in 1987 and is currently an associate professor in Literacy and Secondary English Education at the University of Cincinnati, following 16 years of classroom teaching. Her areas of research and publications involve issues of cross cultural and ethnic literature, young adult prose and poetry, and reading and writing across curriculum, especially mathematics. She is co-editor of a collection of poetry across black cultures—African, African American, and Caribbean. She is listed in *Who's Who in American Education 1992–93*, received the Award of Appreciation for

Outstanding Service to Education by the National Association of University Women. She serves on the Editorial Advisory Board of the *Journal of Reading*.

3

A CONVERSATION WITH PATRICIA AND FREDRICK MCKISSACK

BY ANTHONY L. MANNA AND CAROLYN S. BRODIE

Patricia and Fredrick McKissack presented the keynote address, "Building Bridges With Books," at the eighth annual Virginia Hamilton Conference on April 3, 1992. Our conversations with the McKissacks took place at that time.

M/B: How did you come to write for children?

P.Mc.: Need, just need. Need, in big bold letters. And I will write as long as there continues to be a need. I wanted to introduce my own children to the poetry of Paul Laurence Dunbar, so I went to the library, but there was not one single book in our library about Paul Laurence Dunbar. I wondered, "Why isn't there one?" Dunbar was a great African American poet who gave us beautiful poems. Instead of complaining and moaning about what's not there, I decided to write his biography myself. And so I did.

M/B: How long ago was that?

P.Mc.: 1971.

M/B: You were teaching at that point.

P.Mc.: Yes, I was still teaching. I wrote about Dunbar because there was a need. There was also a need for picture books with children of color. As a child I read a lot, but I was always searching for myself and I didn't find myself in books, and that bothered me. I didn't want that situation to bother other young readers as well. If children don't see themselves in books or have anything that relates to them, soon they won't like to read; that soon becomes *I can't read*, and I can't read means doom.

So I write because there's a need to have books for, by, and about the African American experience and about how we helped to develop this country.

F.Mc.: Talking about need again, Pat likes Dunbar's "Little Brown Baby" because it's one of the few early instances where a black father and a child are shown in such a positive experience.

P.Mc.: And very playful and loving, too. You don't see that image often in children's books. You know, words give us images. What images are our young people getting from television, radio, movie, tapes? How are we writers counteracting that? What are we doing to create positive images so that when children close their eyes they see themselves in positive ways. Too often words like violence, underachiever, poverty—and welfare have become synonyms for African Americans. That's horrible. We need to inspire a generation of writers and illustrators who create positive images. We also need a generation of readers who are going to read to their children.

M/B: Why did you start to read?

P.Mc.: My grandfather. He couldn't read but he loved the idea of reading. And he provided reading material for his family. He bought the newspaper every day, and read it by looking at the pictures and making out what they might mean. He also loved his Bible. He held it. Through the years he had memorized many of the passages. So he quoted it a lot. I loved to hear him quote I John. That's 1st John, but he called it "I John."

M/B: Memory seems important to your life as a writer.

P.Mc.: Memory is very important. Sometimes I start with just a small memory and then embellish it by adding bits and pieces from other events in my life. My own strength comes from my grandparents who were very strong. That's where some of my bad habits come from, too.

M/B: Would you talk about the oral tradition in your own background and how that figures into your writing.

P.Mc.: Writing is an outgrowth of my love of books and words. I heard stories all my life, and I also read stories. People often ask what I read as a child. My favorite book was a collection of mythology. I read Bullfinch long before I was supposed to be able to read and understand those stories. But I read them because I enjoyed them. It was one of the few places where I felt like I was connecting with something. In a lot of the stories I was reading I was looking for an experience that I could relate to and I couldn't do this in the contemporary novels that were being written in the fifties. So I read old stories. I have always loved the way the words were put together.

When Fred and I were growing up, the Nashville Public Library was never segregated. It was one of the few places in Nashville that wasn't. We went in and out of it. We had a respect for books because the librarian respected us. We could go right in the front door. That was quite a thing to be able to do in the South, to go into a large, imposing Carnegie Library as ours was and use the books. So, that was where the love affair with books started. Add all of that to my grandfather's telling tales, my reading to him, and his rich language—all of those things made words very special to me.

M/B: Is it difficult to try to capture the oral feel of a story on the page?

P.Mc.: I had to get beyond language restrictions. As an English major, I was taught to appreciate standard English, e.g., where to put question marks, how to make a complete sentence, verb-subject agreement. I had to throw all of that out and write the way my grandfather talked, in fragments, made-up words, etc. It wasn't easy, but it was fun and much more realistic in my stories.

M/B: You have said the tape recorder is another one of your tools.

P.Mc.: We tape and listen and tape and listen. *A Million Fish…More or Less* came out of that experience. That story is actually one Fred told me.

F.Mc.: It was a joke that I had heard, but Pat changed it. It was actually about a catfish that weighed 500 pounds. Leb and Eb caught a catfish down in the old slough that weighed 500 pounds. So that is what Leb was telling Eb, and Eb didn't want to call Leb a liar. He just said, "What a funny old slough that place is. I was down there and I found a lantern that Ponce de Leon used in 1492 and it was still burning." Well, Eb didn't want to call Leb a liar so

From *A Million Fish…More or Less* by Patricia C. McKissack, illustrated by Dena Schutzer. Illustration copyright © 1992 by Dena Schutzer. Reprinted by permission of Alfred A. Knopf, Inc.

he said to him, "I'll take a few pounds off the catfish, if you put the lantern out."

P.Mc.: He told me that joke and I loved it.

F.Mc.: She recognized it.

P.Mc.: That's the kind of tall tales Daddy James, my grandfather, and Mr. Tinstey, his friend, used to tell all the time. One might say, "He was so strong, he could pick that heavy thing up with one hand." Just exaggerated tales, but then they'd start backing off of them after they made them so wide and so deep; they'd start subtracting some of the pounds. "Did it really weigh 500 pounds?" "Well, give or take a pound." "Was that lantern still burning?" "Well, let's just say it was flickerin' a bit." So what I did was to use Fred's story and by changing it a bit it worked as an introduction to Hugh Thomas's adventure.

M/B: Do you always collaborate in this way?

P.Mc.: Yes, all the time. We talk all the time.

F.Mc.: We have fun with it. We get up at eight o'clock in the morning and we go back to bed at ten or eleven and we tell stories the whole day long. We've come up with an answer for kids who ask us about how stories are created. We tell them that there are two creative processes which come out of literature itself. There's a process where a story literally pops out of your head, just like Athena popped out of the head of Zeus. This is instantaneous creation.

The other one we have named the Mustard Seed type of creation. You get a flicker of an idea—the size of a mustard seed—but it has to grow from an idea to a story or to a book. The idea is there and you just need to keep going back over it. You're driving along and it pops into your head and it grows and grows and grows, and then somewhere along the way you put it down on the word processor and it changes some more.

P.Mc.: *Messy Bessey* was one of those Athena-like ideas that just popped out of our heads fully grown.

F.Mc.: It never was a child.

P.Mc.: It took about an hour to write. We're constantly telling stories to children. Fred and I always told our own kids stories, too, which is part of the African tradition. They taught with stories. They communicated with the great kings with stories, because they couldn't very well tell a king outright that he was wrong. They couldn't tell a ruler that he had made a mistake, and so the storytellers used story to instruct, to influence, to convince, among other things. That's what we try to do with stories.

M/B: And to entertain.

P.Mc.: Oh yes. First to entertain. That's how you get people to listen in the first place.

F.Mc.: We went down to Alabama to Pat's family homeplace for a reunion around 1974 or 1975 or somewhere in that area. One of the old codgers there, who grew up without radio or television, told us stories one night. They were barbecuing in an old-fashioned pit in the ground and everybody sat around the fire. He told his stories there. On our way home we talked the whole time about Uncle B.J.'s stories. We noticed that three-year-olds were smiling and laughing, and so were ten-year-olds, at twenty, and at eighty, too. He told those stories in such a manner that everybody got something out of them.

I think in a sense, Pat tries to tell that type of story where there is a little something for everybody to think about. So a little kid might think of *Flossie and the Fox* in one way and an older person might think of it in another way, but they'd all be entertained. And I think that's important to understand about our history, because that was the way stories were told in slavery times.

P.Mc.: We try to tell our non-fiction in a story voice as well.

M/B: What's your method for doing that?

F.Mc.: I don't think there is a method. The first thing is to pick topics that are of high interest in our community. One of the things that we've talked most about was the 1960s, the era of the sit-ins, the stand-ins, and the wait-ins. Pat and I were part of those events, so we are interested in giving a clear picture of that era. One of the things the reviewer said about *Martin Luther King, Jr.* was that we had overdone the book. We had looked at every word and every phrase to make sure that we were recording and telling the truth.

Pat's office is right next to my office, and we still run from one room to another saying, "Look what I found." We research a lot. First it's the library. We not only go to the public library, we've also built an extensive library of our own on African American issues. Another thing we do is to call old friends to talk about the subjects. Then we have to tie it all together.

P.Mc.: I think it's substance and feeling. We dig constantly, we read constantly. When we go to cities and have a moment, we try to go to museums and libraries and gather bits and pieces of information there. We've found that working on one project gives us an idea for another book.

So a lot of the books we have written are rooted in the civil rights movement. The idea for the James Weldon Johnson book came when we were at the Coretta Scott King breakfast in Chicago. The ceremony started off with "Lift Every Voice" and we looked around and all of the people over forty were singing. They knew the words and seemed to enjoy them. But all the people under forty, and practically all of the whites, couldn't sing the song. They didn't know the words. "Lift every voice and sing, 'till earth and heaven ring, ring with the harmonies of liberty." I said, "Oh Fred, we've got to do a book."

M/B: In that book the hymn has become the structure. That's a beautiful way to go about it.

P.Mc.: That song is an important part of our history. I was speaking with someone yesterday and we laughed about how "Lift Every Voice and Sing" was so important to us, because she lived in one part of the country and I lived in another part of the country, yet our school days started off exactly the same way. We sang "The Star Spangled Banner" and said "The Pledge of Allegiance." Then we said the Lord's Prayer or the Twenty-Third Psalm. And then we sang "Lift Every Voice and Sing," followed by a poem from some great poet. That was the way we started the day.

M/B: Lucky for you, too, because that gave you the rhythm of the language. So many children don't get that because poetry is often considered a special thing for special kids.

F.Mc.: James Weldon Johnson and Paul Laurence Dunbar were good friends.

P.Mc.: Dunbar wrote beautiful poetry in standard English and in black dialect. Johnson was inspired by Dunbar to write "Sence You Went Away,"[1] his first dialect poem.

F.Mc.: Dunbar had died when James Weldon Johnson wrote that poem. James Weldon Johnson and his brother were the first, among the first, that is, to write down the black spirituals, or the Negro spirituals, as they were called at the time. In that book he dedicated each and every song to people like Booker T. Washington, W.E.B. Du Bois, and Paul Laurence Dunbar. When you pick up that book and look at the songs you see so many connections.

P.Mc.: Ideas beget ideas. Most of our books come from work that we did on other books. When we did our biography of W. E. B. Du Bois we were led to Booker T. Washington. They came out of the same era, but they were in conflict with each other.

F.Mc.: And here again, the connections. Dudley Randall, a very famous black poet, wrote about that conflict. We used his poem in the *The Civil Rights Movement in America from 1865 to the Present.* And if you listen to this poem, you'll hear an ongoing conversation in the black community from 1619 to the present day. You want to read it with me, Pat?

F.Mc.: *"It seems to me," said Booker T.,*
"It shows a mighty lot of cheek
To study chemistry and Greek
When Mister Charlie needs a hand
To hoe the cotton on his land,
And when Miss Ann looks for a cook,
Why stick your nose inside a book?"

P.Mc.: *"I don't agree," said W.E.B.*
"If I should have the drive to seek
Knowledge of chemistry or Greek,
I'll do it. Charles and Miss can look
Another place for hand or cook.

Some men rejoice in skill of hand,
And some in cultivating land,
But there are others who maintain
The right to cultivate the brain."

F.Mc.: *"It seems to me," said Booker T.,*
"That all you folks have missed the boat
Who shout about the right to vote,
And spend vain days and sleepless nights
In uproar over civil rights.
Just keep your mouths shut, do not grouse,
But work, and save, and buy a house."

P.Mc.: *"I don't agree," said W.E.B.,*
"For what can property avail
If dignity and justice fail?
Unless you help to make the laws,
They'll steal your house with trumped-up clause.
A rope's as tight, a fire as hot,
No matter how much cash you've got.
Speak soft, and try your little plan,
But as for me, I'll be a man."

F.Mc.: *"It seems to me," said Booker T.*
P.Mc.: *"I don't agree," said W.E.B.*[2]

P.Mc.: That summarizes the conflict that has been going on for a long time even as we speak. You have some blacks who are currently saying, "Hey, we don't need the civil rights movement, it's passé. We don't need affirmative action, we don't need social reform, we don't need those things." Then you have other people who are saying, "Wait a minute, wait a minute, we do need those things." Within the African American community there is conflict and that's why it bothers me when people try to say one black leader represents all black people. We have many, many different leaders and we try to show that in the books we write.

M/B: When you're writing a book like *The Civil Rights Movement in America* what particular angle do you take? This has been done so much, so how do you approach it?

F.Mc.: You've got to keep readers interested in order for them to read anything. In the civil rights book we tell our readers that man's quest for justice didn't begin in the twentieth-century United States. Actually, the story of civil rights has no beginning or end. From ancient times to present, the struggle for rights has been at the core of countless social and political conflicts. But even though the concept for rights is constantly being reevaluated, life and freedom are universally accepted as a basis for human rights. Human rights are the foundation upon which our entire democracy is based. We tell our readers that America itself is founded on the subject of rights which goes back to the time of David and further back still to the story of Adam and Eve. We try to make a connection because the day will come when they will be asked to choose. They'll have to stand up; the trick of it is to stand up for what is right.

P.Mc.: And the best way to know is through reading and gathering information, sorting information, and then coming to conclusions. We felt that our book should not focus entirely on civil rights in African American history. We tried to include the Native American story, we tried to include the Hispanic and Asian story, as well. The struggle for rights among women and immigrants, too, because all of them in turn have had to struggle for their rights. We even included children's stories, because child labor laws were not passed in this country until we had a woman as Secretary of Labor under Roosevelt in the 1930s. Frances Perkins was the first to help push through child labor laws because up until that time children were forced to work in terrible conditions for as little as a dime a day.

M/B: One of the things you remind us of is the split between the spirit and the word.

P.Mc.: What we bring to our subject is the spirit and I think the spirit is what makes the words sing. A lot of people have knowledge of these subjects, they know them very well, but they have difficulty making them interesting to children. And children will not read what they do not enjoy. Let's face it. We can shove it at them, we can test them, we can make it mandatory, we can put it on reading lists from now until forever, but young readers will not read a book if they do not like it. I taught eighth grade English for nine years, and I had trouble trying to get my students to read biography. Then I read some biographies myself and I thought, "No wonder they don't like to read this material. It's awful. It's just listing one dry fact after the other." Very academic and very well researched, but —there was no story, and the people didn't seem real.

Fred's too modest to say, but he digs for the stuff that makes children want to read. I don't like research. Research is tedious. If I can get in the ballpark of the year, that's close enough for me. I'll say, "It happened in 1917." Fred will see 1917 sticking up like a sore thumb and he'll say, "We've got to add some detail to that." So he will go out and find the day, the date, the hour if possible, and he'll even check the weather report and find out if it was raining or sunny that day. So what readers get in our books is that fine detail that you don't usually get in a book, because a lot of people like me would just quit at 1917.

M/B: How did the Pullman Porter book evolve?

P.Mc.: Theirs was a story that needed to be told. You see, it's a wonderful story about a group of men who fought for their rights and made it possible for all black workers to have a little dignity in the jobs they held. It gave other people a reason to stand up later.

M/B: There's a powerful photograph on page 95 of *A Long Hard Journey* of A. Philip Randolph with William Green, who is president of the American Federation of Labor, AFL.

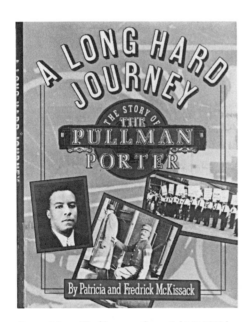

From *A Long Hard Journey*. Copyright © 1989 by Patricia and Fredrick McKissack. Reprinted with permission of Walker & Co.

P.Mc.: That's a very important picture because the Brotherhood of Sleeping Car Porters was the first African American union to be recognized by a major corporation and the first to be an independent brotherhood within the AFL. That's history. It was a fourteen-year struggle. It was incredible what the founding porters went through. They almost lost everything. E. J. Bradley lost his wife because she couldn't take the pressure. She divorced him, and he had to move the Brotherhood office to the trunk of his car. The second Mrs. Bradley is the woman who helped us secure so many of the good photos. She let us borrow

was a rifleman, and he belonged to a rifle club, but she said that during that time he was not hunting for sport, he was hunting to eat. His is just one of the stories of the founding brothers of the Brotherhood of Sleeping Car Porters.

F.Mc.: Look at the photograph on p. 109. Here are Brotherhood

P.Mc.: This has never been in any published book before. But just look at the history here. Adam Clayton Powell and Eleanor Roosevelt; that's a civil rights movement right there.

F.Mc.: It didn't die there either. When they were tearing down the wall in Germany they were singing "We Shall Overcome." Would you have guessed that? Did you know that the first Pullman car was in Abe Lincoln's funeral? Just the crazy connections that you really can never make any sense of, but they are there all the time.

P.Mc.: There are connections in our fiction, too. One of the sections in an upcoming book, *Christmas in the Big House, Christmas in the Quarters*, which will be out in 1993, contains big connections. One of the Christmas foods was "Sweet Potato Pie;" we give the recipe.

Take two sweet potatoes grown in the garden patch outside. Add two cups of sugar. If sugar's not available, use one cup of molasses or honey. One-fourth pound of butter scraped from the inside of the butter churn. Two tablespoons vanilla, one tablespoon of cinnamon, one tablespoon of nutmeg, but if you can't get spices then use a tablespoon of rum. One-fourth cup of milk, if you get to milk a cow. And four eggs. Send the children to gather eggs in the hay.

And then you mix them together and make your pie. When I found this recipe I was in tears, because to make a sweet potato pie, it wasn't like just going out, gathering or buying the ingredients, and making it. They pieced it together, the way black people have always had to piece their lives together from shattered hope and lost dreams. That's the way the cake was made for the cakewalk, too. That's what made the cake the prize. Kids who know *Mirandy and Brother Wind*, wonder about the cake. Why not another prize? You have to show them why that cake is so special, because you had to pilfer, you know, eggs, butter, sugar, from the big house.

From *Mirandy and Brother Wind* by Patricia C. McKissack, illustrated by Jerry Pinkney. Illustration copyright © 1988 by Jerry Pinkney. Reprinted by permission of Alfred A. Knopf, Inc.

F.Mc.: And that's the prize.

M/B: Now we understand that much better, to tell you the truth. Now we understand the social significance of the cake. And who would ever think that there could be a whole world of history in a cake?

P.Mc.: But you know, this is how books happen. I look down at this recipe, and I'm saying, whoa, what a part of history I could do with recipes. Maybe I'll look up more recipes and have a time with story recipes. There are stories in those recipes. The potato pie was the validation for the cakewalk. Because this is how they made the pie, that's how they made the cake. You know, one by one you dig up these things. *Christmas in the Big House, Christmas in the Quarters* tells how Christmas was celebrated in 1859 in Virginia. Now the reason why we chose 1859 is because that's the last time that Christmas would be celebrated in the antebellum South as it was, as it had been, because in 1860 secession would start, and the war would begin, of course, in 1861. The South would never be the same again. So that Christmas had to be a very special one for both slave and master.

F.Mc.: It was also the Christmas of Harpers Ferry.

P.Mc.: Robert E. Lee defeated John Brown, so naturally there would have been a lot of talk in Virginia about that incident. Of course, the underground railroad was very active at that time. It's the changing of history, changing from the old South to the coming of freedom. The reason why we chose the state of Virginia is because Virginia is the mother of the American Christmas. Christmas was first celebrated in Virginia. The eastern colonies didn't celebrate Christmas. In fact, it was forbidden among the Puritans, and a person could be fined for even feasting at Christmas.

But the Virginians always celebrated Christmas, both slave and master. Many of our present-day traditions come from the big house. The drinking of eggnog, for example. The Christmas tree which came from Germany was first brought to Williamsburg,

Virginia. There were also the slave traditions of celebrating Christmas, using red and green for example. Those were slave colors, because red was an easy dye to make, and greenery came from the woodland.

F.Mc.: There are some personal connections in *The Dark Thirty*, another new book of ours.

P.Mc.: When I was growing up and we were playing in the yard, [at the end of the day] we would look up at the sky at the twilight hour, and call it the *dark-thirty*, because we had thirty minutes to get home before it got dark and the monsters came out. So these are stories that have an odd twist to them. Again, I've taken historical events and written around them.

In "Woman in the Snow" I created a ghost that haunts a local bus at about the time of the Montgomery Bus Boycott. There's another story that happens during the death of Martin Luther King, that horrible period when King was killed, and then Robert F. Kennedy was killed within months. All of the stories are based on historical events. Perhaps you'd like to hear one of the stories to give you a flavor of the way they sound. This is called "The Chicken Coop Monster."

When I was nine my parents' ten-year marriage dissolved. Nobody really wanted to talk about divorce in those days. They whispered about it in hushed tones, so I had to define it my own way. I defined divorce to mean if my parents didn't love each other, then they didn't love me. I carried all my hurt and anger and frustration inside.

My parents shipped me off to Nashville to be with my grandparents, and I hated the whole idea. As soon as I walked onto their place I knew that a monster lived in the chicken coop. I knew that he was there, because I could feel his hot red eyes watching me when I played. When I got too close to that old coop I could smell its foul breath, so I knew it was there. One evening my grandmother said to me, "Pat, the chicken coop door is open, would you please go out and close it?" It was at the hour called the dark thirty. It was neither light nor dark. It's when things change and the mind plays tricks on the eyes and you think that it's a tree branch, but it could be the arm of a monster reaching out. I wasn't about to go near that chicken coop at that hour because that's when the monster is strongest. So I stood there frozen in terror and my grandmother said, "Pat, haven't you gone and shut that door for me?" and I said, "No, I'm not going out there." "What do you mean," she said, "you're not going out there; of course you're going out there to close that door." "No," I said, "There's a monster out there." "Oh, girl, don't be silly. There's no such thing as a monster." You see, that's how monsters work, they fool adults. They make you think that they don't exist. Well she said, "If you don't go close that door, something will get in and trouble my chickens." I hated to be the one to tell her but there was already something in there and that's why I didn't want to go.

She was going to drag me out there. I broke away from her, ran into the house, screaming and crying. That's when I felt strong— very, very strong—arms patting me on my back. It was my grand-father, Daddy James, and he said, "What troubles you so about that old chicken coop?" And I said, "It's a monster in there." "Oh? Tell me about your monster," he said. Aha, my grandfather didn't say there's no such thing as a monster. He asked me what my monster looked like. Was he a believer? I had to check it out. "Daddy James, do you believe in monsters? Mama Frances says they don't exist." He said, "Oh, you know monsters are like that, they try to make you think that they don't exist, but, oh yes, I know they do." He had asked me to describe my monster. Of course, I had never seen my monster. I didn't know what he looked like really, but I guess if it lived in the chicken coop, it must look like a chicken, right? It must have big claws, clawed feet, it must have a long beak that was pointed, and instead of having just the regular feathers on its back, it had scales. And big red eyes. So I described my monster.

My grandpa said, "You know, there used to be a monster that lived in the crawl space under my house, too. And that old monster used to just scare me to death. Had me so scared I couldn't even play in my own front yard." "You did?" And he said, "The only way I could get rid of him was to call him out." "To call him out? You called out a monster?" "Yep." "Did you win?" "Yep, I whipped him good and sent him right back to monsterland." "Well, good, will you go and do something about the monster that lives in your chicken coop?" "No," he said, "I can't do that. That's your monster and you've got to call out your own monster." "But I'm just a little girl," I said. "Well, I was just a little boy. Now with some monsters you can face them, you have to be strong and just believe that you can beat them. And you know the stronger you get, the weaker that monster will get."

Well armed with the only thing I had I went out to face my monster and I called him out. And the creaky old door swung open and I thought, nope, this is not a good decision. I started to run, but then I thought about what my grandfather said. If I stayed strong the monster would leave, so I called him out and I said, "Monster, come on out, it's me and I'm not afraid of you." Of course, I was terrified. "Come on out," I said. "I am the oldest granddaughter of James Leon Oldham and he loves me and I know it."   That monster left. The point is that if we create our own monsters, we also have to face them.

M/B: In your presentation at the Virginia Hamilton Conference you said that your female characters are the daughters you always wanted, considering that your children are males.

P.Mc.: Those are my daughters, all right. They are the outgrowth of me. They can't be me totally because I never did all those wonderful things, like catch the wind or outsmart a fox, but if I had daughters, that's how I would want them to be able to react to problems, that's how I'd want them to make decisions and solve problems. Now, naturally, I have set them in very tight situations, but I think you can guess the kind of upbringing they had by the way they act. So in a way that's me and that's where the "me" comes through.

M/B: They're all survivors.

F.Mc.: There's a statement in the black community that you hear all the time. It says, "Keep on keepin on."

M/B: That's central in all of your books.

F.Mc.: Keep on keepin on.

P.Mc.: I love that. We never give up, we find a way.

M/B: That's a beautiful message to give to people, in general, and to children, in particular.

P.Mc.: Find a way, find a way. You know, that's the real struggle isn't it? It's a struggle for all of us and I think to me that's the key to what we call multiculturalism, because that's one of the ways in which we all become a parallel culture, as Virginia Hamilton says.

F.Mc.: We do things more alike than we do them differently. The more you talk to people, the more you find that out.

NOTES:

1. Johnson, "Sence You Went Away," in *Fifty Years & Other Poems*, 63.

2. Randall, "Booker T. and W.E.B.," in *Black Poetry*, 16.

WORKS CITED:

Johnson, James Weldon. *Fifty Years & Other Poems*. Boston: The Cornhill Company, 1917.

Randall, Dudley, ed. *Black Poetry*. Detroit: Broadside Press, 1969.

A SELECTED LISTING
OF BOOKS BY PATRICIA AND FREDRICK MCKISSACK

Louis Armstrong: Jazz Musician. Hillside, NJ: Enslow Publishers, 1991.

The Civil Rights Movement in America from 1865 to the Present. Chicago: Childrens Press, 1987.

George Washington Carver: The Peanut Scientist. Hillside, NJ: Enslow Publishers, 1991.

Frederick Douglass: The Black Lion. Chicago: Childrens Press, 1987.

Fredrick Douglass: Leader Against Slavery. Hillside, NJ: Enslow Publishers, 1991.

W. E. B. Du Bois. New York: Franklin Watts, 1990.

James Weldon Johnson: Lift Every Voice & Sing. Chicago: Childrens Press, 1990.

A Long Hard Journey: The Story of the Pullman Porter. New York: Walker & Co., 1990.

Martin Luther King, Jr.: Man of Peace. Hillside, NJ: Enslow Publishers, 1991.

Messy Bessey. Illustrated by Richard Hackney. Chicago: Childrens Press, 1987.

Carter G. Woodson: The Father of Black History. Hillside, NJ: Enslow Publishers, 1991.

A SELECTED LISTING
OF BOOKS BY PATRICIA MCKISSACK

The Dark Thirty: Southern Tales of the Supernatural. New York: Knopf, 1992.

Paul Laurence Dunbar: A Poet to Remember. Chicago: Childrens Press, 1984.

Flossie and the Fox. Illustrated by Rachel Isadora. New York: Dial, 1986.

The Inca. Chicago: Childrens Press, 1985.

Los Incas. Chicago: Childrens Press, 1987.

King Midas and His Gold. Illustrated by Tom Dunnington. Chicago: Childrens Press, 1986.

The Maya. Chicago: Childrens Press, 1985.

Los Mayas. Chicago: Childrens Press, 1987.

A Million Fish...More or Less. Illustrated by Dena Schutzer. New York: Knopf, 1992.

Mirandy and Brother Wind. Illustrated by Jerry Pinkney. New York: Knopf, 1988.

Monkey-Monkey's Trick. Illustrated by Paul Meisel. New York: Random House, 1988.

Nettie Jo's Friends. Illustrated by Scott Cook. New York: Knopf, 1989.

(With Ruthilde Kronberg). *A Piece of the Wind and Other Stories to Tell*. San Francisco: Harper San Francisco, 1990.

ABOUT THE MCKISSACKS

Since 1975 Patricia and Fredrick McKissack have collaborated on more than 40 books, including *The Civil Rights Movement in America* and *Frederick Douglass: The Black Lion*. In addition to winning a C. S. Lewis Silver Award in 1985 for *Abram, Abram, Where Are You Going?*, the McKissacks received the Coretta Scott King Award in 1989 for *A Long Hard Journey: The Story of the Pullman Porter*, which was also named a Notable Book by both the American Library Association and the National Council on Social Studies-Children's Book Council. A former editor of children's books, Patricia McKissack also has written a series on American Indian cultures, biographies of Mary McLeod Bethune, Paul Laurence Dunbar, and Martin Luther King, Jr., and several highly acclaimed picture books. *Flossie and the Fox* is based on a folktale told to her by her grandfather, and *Mirandy and Brother Wind*, which Jerry Pinkney illustrated, was named a Caldecott Honor Book in 1990 and received the Coretta Scott King Award for illustration. *A Million Fish...More or Less* is an original tall tale set in the Bayou Clapateaux. The McKissacks are the owners of All-Writing Services, a family business located in Clayton, Missouri. They are the parents of three sons.

4

MAKING THE JOURNEY

BY SHEILA HAMANAKA

The Journey is a book I wrote about the incarceration of Japanese Americans during World War II. After the war broke out with Japan the United States rounded up all of the Japanese Americans on the West Coast, some 110,000 of them, and put them into concentration camps. There were ten of them. My parents were in a camp in Jerome, Arkansas, for several years. I didn't know about this when I was growing up. Occasionally I would hear my parents talking about camp. Many of my generation would say their parents talked about camp, some of us thought they were talking about summer camp. It wasn't until the late 1960s, when I was actively protesting the injustices of the Vietnam War, that I began to think about the fact that my own parents had been in a concentration camp. To tell you the truth, it was terribly embarrassing to admit that I didn't know very much about something this significant.

In the late 1980s I applied for a grant from the Japanese American Citizens' League so that I could create a mural that explains Japanese American history. Although *The Journey* was published as a children's book, the mural itself was not painted for children. It became a children's book by accident. One day my editor, Dick Jackson paid me a visit and saw the mural in my living room. It's pretty big. It measures twenty-five feet across. He looked at it for a long time and offered me a contract on the spot to make it into a children's book. I spent about a year doing the research for the imagery in the mural. I went down to the National Archives in Washington, D.C. The Archives contain about 10,000 photographs taken by the government which document the experiences of the Japanese American concentration camps before, during, and after the internment. Some of the photographers became very well-known like Dorothea Lange and Ansel Adams.

The mural is painted in oil, and it is done in five large panels.

The first panel largely shows the work Japanese Americans did when they first came to this country. You see people fishing, because the Japanese Americans helped to build the tuna and abalone fishing industries. The men are fishing for tuna off the back of the boat with six foot poles. They just fling the fish behind them into the boat. Next to the fishermen are cannery workers and "stoop laborers."

The "stoop laborers" would spend their entire day crawling through the fields on their hands and knees as they picked produce. The woman in the center is a farm worker. She is overlooking what is going on. The woman who posed for me, whose name is Emi Tonooka, told me that her mother was a farm worker, and that when she was a little girl she had to massage her mother's back because she was so tired from working in the fields. Emi herself had a nervous breakdown in the concentration camp when she was a teenager.

In the background of the first panel there are scenes from Little Tokyo, painted in black and white.

Panel One. Illustrations by Sheila Hamanaka from *The Journey* by Sheila Hamanaka. Copyright © 1990 by Sheila Hamanaka. Used with permission of the publisher, Orchard Books, New York.

Little Tokyo, like the Chinatowns in this country, arose because of segregation, although it might be considered a picturesque neighborhood now. Like the Chinese Americans the Japanese Americans were not allowed to own any property in the United States, so sometimes they put property in the name of their children. It was illegal for them to marry European Americans. When the war broke out people would put up a sign on their stores to try to identify themselves as Americans, but it didn't work. Many of them lost quite a bit of money and property. There was also the emotional stress. Sometimes their neighbors figured that, well, these people are moving out anyway, so why should we buy their stuff. They can't take the stuff with them. So they would wait until these people left and then just steal their possessions. Japanese Americans were forced to sell everything they owned. They were given anywhere from two days to two weeks to liquidate all of their assets to pay off their debts, and as you can imagine they were taken advantage of.

Above the towering farm worker in the first panel you see human figures rendered as Bunraku puppets. I've painted Franklin Delano Roosevelt as well as political and military figures of the time as puppets. Not very many people know it, but FDR was racist. He thought that the Japanese had a different kind of cranial structure and this made them inferior to whites. He thought you could get over this problem by interbreeding the Japanese with Europeans. He had a professor at the Smithsonian working on this plan. Two-thirds of the people who were put in camps were American citizens, and the way the government got around the Constitution was that they declared the West Coast a military theater of operations.

In the first panel I also depicted the first four people who challenged their imprisonment in the camps. As in other sections of the mural I used a theatrical theme to show their struggle before the court. The masks they are wearing are images from Japanese Noh drama. I see history as theater. It's taught as reality, but to me it's theater because it's somebody's story, and it's always an interpretation of the facts. Also court, is a form of theater, so I painted the

Supreme Court as a chorus, and the petitioners behind them are assuming the traditional pose of enlightenment. These figures are enlightened to the fact that they really don't have any rights in front of the court. As it turned out, they lost their cases. In fact, it wasn't until the late 1980s that most of the cases were vacated.

Of course, children also were put in the camps. My two brothers and my sister were in a concentration camp. Two of the children I painted in the mural are saluting the flag. You can see them next to the puppet politicians and military men in the first panel. Concerning the children that were incarcerated, I recently heard a very sad story about a mother in the camps who had a thirty-two year old son who was retarded. She cared for him all the time on her farm. They told her she couldn't bring him to the camp because they couldn't take care of him, so they had to institutionalize him. A month after she got to the camp she received a letter saying that he had died.

Children went to school at the camps. My mother is still in touch with a woman who taught in these schools. She said that the children were very quiet and they seemed depressed. They didn't understand what was happening to them. The camps, of course, were surrounded by barbed wire, and many former inmates have reported that they were told they were put in concentration camps for their own protection because Americans would attack them. Yet, when they got to camp they noticed that all of the machine guns were pointed inward at them. If you went too close to the barbed wire fences you could be shot. In fact, several people were shot and killed, including older people who would just wander too close to the fences. Some people were shot from walking too slowly. In one incident a soldier was fined for killing an inmate. He was fined a dollar, which was the cost of the bullet he used.

In the second panel I show an ancient Japanese theater where the seating for the audience is sunk into the floor. The audience here consists of politicians and journalists of the period who are wearing masks. The configuration in the background is a rebellion at Manzanar where inmates were shot and killed. They were rebelling partly because some people who worked for the administration had been stealing food from the kitchen.

I also put the Ku Klux Klan in the second panel. I did this because in the United States racist attacks were not only made against the Japanese. It was a period of great racism in this country. Even the armed forces were segregated. Right after the war, in fact, there was a lynching wave that went on in the South.

In the second frame of the mural I also placed references to the Nuremberg trials. This I did because the Nazis at the Nuremberg trials—to justify what they did to the Jews—used as their defense what the Americans had done to the Japanese. You see Nazi leaders in this scene. You also see Walter Lippmann. He's there because many liberals, as well as right-wingers, were opposed to the Japanese. In fact, the American Civil Liberties Union supported the con-

Panel Two. Illustrations by Sheila Hamanaka from *The Journey* by Sheila Hamanaka. Copyright © 1990 by Sheila Hamanaka. Used with permission of the publisher, Orchard Books, New York.

centration camps. There was only one chapter on the West Coast that tried to defend the Japanese.

In the third panel I pay tribute to the Spanish painter Goya, both his style and his political awareness. In December of 1942 U.S. military police opened fire on Japanese American protestors at the Manzanar Relocation Center in California. Two protestors died and eight were wounded. Some of the people in this panel are running away, representing the Japanese Americans who were disillu-

Panels Three and Four. Illustrations by Sheila Hamanaka from *The Journey* by Sheila Hamanaka. Copyright © 1990 by Sheila Hamanaka. Used with permission of the publisher, Orchard Books, New York.

sioned with America and want to repatriate to Japan. Some 8,000 actually left.

In the fourth panel I continued the theater motif. In this case, people of my generation are holding Western-style masks to indicate the influence of Western culture in their lives. When I studied art history in high school it did not include Asian culture, African culture, or Latin American culture. My characters are therefore holding Western-style masks and thinking about their own acculturation. Of course, some of them are not willing to look at the past. In this panel, however, some people are documenting their past such as the woman holding the video camera. This is something we all need to do. Rewriting and redocumenting history are necessary if we hope to ever understand our own past. At the bottom of this panel is a woman who is mourning for her son who was killed in the war. The figures around her are assuming Noh poses of enlightenment and extreme grief.

At the top of the fourth panel is a depiction of the atomic bombs that were dropped on Japan in 1945. I personally feel that one of the reasons the United States dropped the atomic bomb on Japan was because the people were Japanese; they simply were different. The Japanese Americans were allowed to join the army to fight in the war. There were about 33,000 of these soldiers. In this panel Japanese American soldiers are also shown liberating the inmates at Dachau—a kind of irony considering that many of their own parents were in concentration camps in this country. Next to the Dachau survivors are soldiers returning from the war. Above them is another Noh mask. One of the Noh masks in this panel is of Yoroboshi, a kind of prodigal son among the Noh drama characters. He was wrongfully banished from his home. I have used him to symbolize the Japanese Americans who returned to Japan after the war because they were totally disillusioned. Later, many of them tried to return to the States. Some of those who returned to Japan were separated from their families for as long as fifteen years. When they did come back to the States they found a lot of racism, Japanese cemeteries defiled, their homes taken over, and so on. With my own family, my father's parents had a home in Fresno,

California. My grandfather died in a concentration camp, probably from lack of adequate medical care. Their home was left in the care of a minister, but when my grandmother returned to claim the family home, the minister refused to give it over to her. A court battle ensued.

This is the final panel. In previous panels the puppets were controlled by unseen forces. Here you have people controlling their own puppets, a sign of their empowerment. In the back-

Panel Five. Illustrations by Sheila Hamanaka from *The Journey* by Sheila Hamanaka. Copyright © 1990 by Sheila Hamanaka. Used with permission of the publisher Orchard Books, New York.

ground there are scenes of contemporary Little Tokyo, in Los Angeles, where Japanese activists are seeking reparation. Scores of citizens' committees, like the National Council for Japanese American Redress, sprouted up around the country to wage a national campaign for reparation. The paper crane near the center of the panel is a symbol of the *hibakusha*, the name given to survivors of the atomic bomb blasts.

The content of the final panel shows much hope. For example, activists are being led by the *yonsei*, the fourth generation, and the little boy holding the peach fulfills the promise of the laborer in the first panel, who is also holding a peach. He is looking to a better future; this child is the future. The boy in the foreground wears a tee-shirt with a wave on it, a symbol of power and resilience, while the man to the viewer's right wears a shirt that bears sparrows, a symbol of the repayment of debt. The carp that appears in this panel symbolizes renewal. You see, after much debate and lobbying on the part of Japanese Americans and their many supporters, the government finally apologized in 1988. The survivors of the camps were promised $20,000 each.

There are many lessons in history. Because the Supreme Court has never declared the camps unconstitutional, it is still possible for this thing to happen again. Congressman Norman Mineta said that the FBI briefed Congress at the beginning of the Gulf War, saying that there were camps in Louisiana that were ready to hold Arabs and their sympathizers. I connect the bombing of Hiroshima and Nagasaki, where over 20,000 people were killed, with the bombing of Iraq, where they dropped the equivalent of fifteen atomic bombs and killed up to 200,000. It's a little more sophisticated now, but the racist hysteria raised before the bombing of Iraq is similar in my mind to the racist hysteria created during World War II.

What is hopeful about the future is that we have gatherings like the Virginia Hamilton Conference where we can discuss phenomena like the camps. We also have people writing books that tell children the truth. I have met teachers who were very responsive to *The Journey*, and very concerned about what their students were learning. The children themselves are also very open-minded about these issues. Hopefully, things will get better.

A SELECTED LISTING OF BOOKS BY SHEILA HAMANAKA

Chortles: New & Selected Wordplay Poems. Written by Eve Merriam. Illustrated by Sheila Hamanaka. New York: Morrow, 1989.

Class Clown. Written by Johanna Hurwitz. Illustrated by Sheila Hamanaka. New York: Morrow, 1987.

Class President. Written by Johanna Hurwitz. Illustrated by Sheila Hamanaka. New York: Morrow, 1990.

The Journey: Japanese Americans, Racism & Renewal. Written and illustrated by Sheila Hamanaka. New York: Orchard Books, 1990.

Molly the Brave & Me. Written by Jane O'Connor. Illustrated by Sheila Hamanaka. New York: Random House, 1990.

A Poem for a Pickle: Funnybone Verses. Written by Eve Merriam. Illustrated by Sheila Hamanaka. New York: Morrow, 1989.

Teacher's Pet. Written by Johanna Hurwitz. Illustrated by Sheila Hamanaka. New York: Morrow, 1988.

ABOUT THE AUTHOR

Sheila Hamanaka is an award-winning artist whose work has been exhibited throughout the country. *The Journey*, the first book she both wrote and illustrated, is based upon her parents' internment in a concentration camp for Japanese Americans. She is also the illustrator of *The Terrible Eek*, a Japanese folktale retold by Patricia A. Compton. "Making *The Journey*" is adapted from the slide presentation she made as a featured speaker at the seventh annual Virginia Hamilton Conference on April 5, 1991. Sheila Hamanaka lives with her son and daughter in Tappan, New York.

5

A JOURNEY TOWARD A COMMON GROUND
THE STRUGGLE AND IDENTITY OF HISPANICS IN THE U.S.A.

BY NICHOLASA MOHR

As a daughter of a Puerto Rican diaspora, I was born and raised in an urban village nestled in the heart of New York City. I grew up unaware that throughout the United States there existed many barrios similar to Manhattan's Spanish Harlem. I had no idea that I had an extended Hispanic family living in Chicago, Tampa, Los Angeles, and in a multitude of towns and cities all across this nation, or that we shared a common culture. Just like my family, who lived in Spanish Harlem, they spoke both Spanish and English, shopped in the bodegas, ate plantains with rice and beans, listened to Spanish radio programs, attended mass in Spanish, and perhaps the children, like myself, might have even attempted to read our parents' copy of the Spanish daily newspapers. Back then, in the 1940s and 1950s, most Hispanics stayed in their neighborhoods. The only way to achieve acceptance and a chance to be in the mainstream of this society was to not only embrace the local American culture, but also to reject one's own Hispanic culture. This attempt at assimilation, this frustrating struggle to fit in, was encouraged. It was reinforced in the schools by social workers and most authority figures outside our community. For most of us growing up then, it was a time when success meant acceptance into that European culture that dominated these United States. All too often, the price of this success was paid by discarding our own history and never seeking the truth of our past. Anglo-American values demanded that we had to reject our parents' language and change our way of thinking. Even our clothes and food were seen to be foreign.

Going as far as changing our name from Jivera to Rivers wasn't such a bad idea either. In fact it made it easier when you went looking for an apartment in a better Anglo neighborhood. Assimilation as defined by the Anglo society was a primary focus —the aspiration and the ultimate goal of an Hispanic child who expected to make it in the dominant system. And in the movies and television, newspapers and magazines, and on the radio, it was validated that this was the only way to be a true American. Hispanics, along with blacks, were seen in menial roles or depicted as crude stereotypes such as Frito Bandito and the lazy Mexican. Spanish was never heard; our people were never seen as we really were; our stories were never told. There was a rhyme that many of us kids in the streets of New York recited. To my knowledge, it was originated by African Americans in the South. Our variation follows:

> *If you're white, you're right;*
> *If you're yellow, you're mellow;*
> *If you're brown, hang around;*
> *If you're black, step back;*
> *If you're just Spanish, you'll be banished.*

This rhyme rang true for those of us who fit these descriptions.

Schools provided either nothing or a distorted sense of our own history. As Puerto Ricans we knew we were not only different from Anglos, but we were also different from other Latinos. First we were born citizens. Even the island of Puerto Rico which was owned by the United States was not a real country, we were informed. I learned in the public schools in New York City that it was the benevolent Americans who saved us from the cruel Spaniards and in a sense adopted us. We, in turn, should be grateful, speak only English and strive toward total acceptance.

There were no positive role models for me out there in the Great Society when I was growing up. When I searched with a need to emulate a living person—preferably a woman with whom I could identify—my efforts were futile. As a Puerto Rican female in the U.S., my legacy was one of either a negative image or invisibility. My knowledge of myself, of the history of the Puerto Rican people, and of the Hispanic contribution to the United States were to come later when I would seek and find those works and books that held the truth. From the outset, first as a visual artist early in my career and later as I began to write, I understood that the source of my output had to come from within my community. As a female Puerto Rican coming from a long line of strong, determined women, I was not going to be a party to the stereotyping that existed—in particular the stereotype of the Spanish woman that I call the Maria syndrome. Maria the Virgin, or Maria the Magdalena.

The Maria syndrome was even immortalized in that great American classic *West Side Story*: beautiful music, exquisite dancing, the entire production conceived, arranged, choreographed, and presented by successful white males—not one of them Hispanic. Here we have Maria the Virgin ready to sacrifice all. On the other side, the Latino Anita, a loose one who said, "I want to live in America, not in Puerto Rico. That ain't America. It ain't good enough." In the old black and white movies, we had the famous Carmen Miranda dancing on mountains of tropical fruits, and there was always the prostitute —sometimes disguised as a dancer or sexy performer— and the virgin offering, often the sacrificing mother.

Where were the rest of us? Where were my mother and aunt and all those valiant women who had left Puerto Rico out of necessity, for the most part, by themselves, bringing small children to a cold and hostile city? They came with thousands of others driven out by poverty, ill-equipped, with little education, and no knowledge of English. But they were determined to give their children a better life and hope for the future. This is where I had come from, and it was these women who became my heroes. When I look for subjects to paint and stories to write, and I look for role models that symbolize strength, I have only to look at my own and my source is boundless—my folklore is rich and the work to be done consumes an eternity. It was that sense of being invisible in society that I felt while growing up, that has compelled me to produce a body of work that will confront the reader with the truth of my existence and my communities' impact on the larger society.

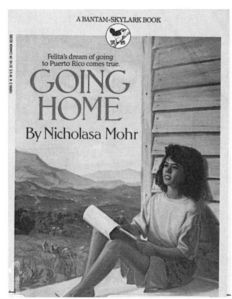

From *Going Home* (Jacket Cover) by Nicholasa Mohr. Copyright © 1986 by Nicholasa Mohr. Used by permission of Bantam Books, a division of Bantam Books, a division of Bantam Doubleday Dell Publishing Group, Inc.

Much of this awakening began as we entered the 1960s as the black social revolution swept the rest of the ethnic minorities into confronting political and racial issues—issues that for generations had been ignored or rejected by our government and elected officials. And with these confrontations came the trials of self-examination. The question of whether Puerto Ricans and other Spanish-speaking Americans were black or white was posed. For the first time, Mexican Americans, Puerto Ricans, Cuban Americans—in fact, any persons coming in from Spanish speaking countries—were all classified as Hispanic Americans. Being black or white created a dilemma for many Hispanic families, where one child was white and the other brown, such as my own, or where the pigmentation of one's skin was academic. We were now—whether blond, brown or black, whether immigrant or migrant—all Hispanics. As Puerto Ricans we had an identity across this vast nation that would unite us with other Hispanics in numbers and geography, and thus this new status gave us greater political clout and began to establish cultural bonds with our Hispanic family throughout the U.S. Out of this new awareness came frustration, anger, marches, demonstrations, and sit-ins. The results of these efforts helped to create such opportunities as open enrollment, affirmative action, and bilingual education. Puerto Rican history began to be taught in the schools and colleges. Sadly, we know that some of these programs have been discontinued and others are being threatened, but the impact and awareness remain.

Inevitably we began to question who we were and how similar we were, coming from such a variety of Spanish-speaking countries. Classifying people with so many different nationalities as one group can cause confusion. After all, outside the United States we were Cuban, Mexican, Chilean, but here, whether one came from the sophisticated metropolis of Buenos Aires, Argentina, or the village of Mocha in the highlands of the Dominican Republic, we were now classified as members of one Hispanic community.

Invariably, it is and will be easier for the children who are born and raised in the United States to accept and understand what it means to be an Hispanic American and to belong to that particular ethnic group. It is from this rich and varied Latino culture that we now share, that a new American ethnic consciousness has erupted. Its manifestations are becoming visible and evident, and it is because of this that we have writers, musicians, and film makers who began out of necessity to create an informal hegemony in arts and letters. We now have dance and theater companies, magazines, and small presses. An example is Arte Publico Press. Arte Publico is the press that publishes Latino writers who would otherwise be ignored by the American literary establishment. The results in terms of works produced reflect our common ground which is indeed an Hispanic experience. And it is mostly ours. It is from this peculiar position in American history that my work has evolved.

I would like briefly to share my role as a writer. Back in 1972, I was asked to write a novel based on a short number of vignettes that I had completed. It was then that I decided that if I as a woman in my ethnic community did not exist in North American letters, I would now. In 1973, Harper & Row published my first novel, *Nilda*. Although much of this story comes from the realms of my imagination, nonetheless, like so many writers' first books, it contains a great deal of autobiographical material. In this book I was able to unlock the memories and sensibilities of my early years. I was able to document what it was to be poor, female, and Puerto Rican in an alien environment. Survival, after all, must not be all our children should strive for. They must be allowed to thrive and to continue to explore their God-given talents. I felt the need to continue and write about my community—women, the children, the heart of my culture. And I'm still at it, exploring and never ceasing to be amazed at the human capacity for endurance and peoples' ability to surprise and disarm.

The challenge to work and document events that unfold within my community with its varied players, its complex and ever-changing position, fires me on to work with a gusto that I could only feel in writing about what I really know and truly care about. Today as I work I no longer feel that sense of isolation I did growing up, and when I'm invited to a conference honoring and recognizing someone like Virginia Hamilton it makes me proud. I'm also very pleased to be here sharing this time with my other co-workers and artists, writers here who are women of color. I know there are some of us out there doing something right—working and producing for our children, trying to make significant changes, providing positive role models for our young people.

I leave you with this final thought. Our children deserve to have that pride in themselves and their community that was missing from many of our own lives as youngsters. Those that follow us do not have to be outcasts in their own lands. All of us go forward. Let's take that responsibility and run with it. Let's validate and celebrate not only what we have managed to accomplish, but all that we must do and build in the years ahead. Let us continue to fight in order to insure our rightful place in society and commit to a positive legacy for all of our children.

A SELECTED LISTING OF BOOKS BY NICHOLASA MOHR:

El Bronx Remembered. 2nd ed. Houston: Arte Publico Press, 1986.

Felita. Illustrated by Ray Cruz. New York: Dial Books for Young People, 1979.

Going Home. New York: Dial Books for Young People, 1986.

In Nueva York. New York: Dial Books for Young People, 1977.

Nilda. 2nd ed. Houston: Arte Publico Press, 1986.

Rituals of Survival: a Woman's Portfolio. Houston: Arte Publico Press, 1985.

ABOUT THE AUTHOR

Nicholasa Mohr is an artist, novelist, teacher, media writer/ producer, and a vital voice in American literature from within the Puerto Rican community. Her work includes *Nilda*, *El Bronx Remembered*, *In Nueva York*, *Going Home*, *Felita*, and *Rituals of Survival: A Woman's Portfolio*. She has received the Jane Addams Book Award, the American Book Award, the Edgar Allan Poe Award, and an Honorary Doctorate from the State University of New York at Albany. She has said, "From the moment my mother handed me some scrap paper, a pencil, and a few crayons, I discovered that by making pictures and writing letters I could create my own world...like "magic." In the small crowded apartment I shared with my large family, making "magic" permitted me all the space, freedom, and adventure that my imagination could handle.... With this "magic" I can recreate those deepest of personal memories as well as validate and celebrate my heritage and my future."

6

THE MYTHIC DIMENSIONS OF APPALACHIA

BY GARY D. SCHMIDT

At the beginning of *Where the Lilies Bloom* an unnamed traveler descends out of the Great Smoky Mountains as if descending from the sky itself, and tells the children gathered around him that he has been in the mountains "for the memory."[1] It is a mythic moment; the mysterious and unknowable oracle descends to the people to make a pronouncement. And it is a pronouncement pregnant with imagery: "This is fair land; the fairest I have ever seen."[2] The traveler disappears, not to reappear in the novel. But the pronouncement, made before any of the plot situations of the book even begin to develop, stays with the reader and informs the rest of the action. Though it is not Eden, and though cruel frosts and cruel people might reach through the wooded slopes, it is a fair land.

It is a land that many have called fair. One of the largest mountain systems of North America, Appalachia extends from the St. Lawrence Valley in Quebec to the coastal plains of Alabama. The most common understanding of Appalachia, however, does not include the extreme ends, but focuses on the central mountain ranges, the Allegheny Mountains of Virginia and West Virginia, the Black Mountains, the Blue Ridge of the Carolinas, and the Great Smoky Mountains that rise into Tennessee. In dealing with Appala-

This article is based on a workshop Professor Schmidt presented at the 1992 Virginia Hamilton Conference, it is adopted from "Appalachian Spring" *The Five Owls*, June 1991, pp. 107-109.

chia, these are the areas where children's literature has set its tales.

But the opening to *Where the Lilies Bloom* does more than announce the setting; it announces that this novel will be participating in the myth of Appalachia, a vision of this region which is surprisingly consistent in the many genres in which it appears in children's literature. Whether the myth of the region is true factually is less important than whether it is true mythically, whether it reaches towards expressing something of the spirit of the region. Very diverse writers of children's literature have found in that spirit something which has a universal dimension—an important element of any myth. And so writers have used the myth of Appalachia to speak to the child audience of the beauty of the world and of its hardships, of the need for self-reliance and the need for community, of tenacity and sheer guts and of wonder at the simplest moments of the child's life.

Perhaps the strongest element of the Appalachian myth is the physical splendor of this world. Central to the myth is a celebration of the beauty of the Appalachians themselves, a beauty so permanent and so eternal that even Mary Call's doubts that spring will return in *Where the Lilies Bloom* are never taken seriously. In this novel it is a beauty which is intimate, so that the names of the surrounding mountains are not mere geographical tags, but the names of familiars: Sugar Boy and Old Joshua and Three Top.

Two of the books set in this region use the region's beauty to organize the entire narrative. Diane Goode's illustrations for Cynthia Rylant's *When I Was Young in the Mountains* picture the mountains of West Virginia from the perspective of the young child. Things which might not seem beautiful to an adult—a dark and muddy swimming hole, a well pump down below the house, a black snake sliding through the yard—are infinitely intriguing to a child. The narrator finds every element of her life caught up with the natural world around her, whether it be her grandfather working in the coal mine, the shooting stars that cross over her cabin, or baptisms in the swimming hole.

Warren Ludwig's *Good Morning, Granny Rose* also uses the beauty of the mountains to organize the narrative. When Granny Rose sets off with her beagle for a morning walk through the winter forest, she is clearly on a daily journey through splendid woods. The center of the book is a wordless two-page spread of Granny Rose and her beagle sitting on a cliff's edge, overlooking soft hills whose rounded peaks reflect the shape of the sun as it just rises above them. By the last illustration, as Granny Rose comes down off the mountain, her cabin is as much a part of the landscape as the two spruces in the foreground.

But this world, though beautiful, is also filled with natural perils. The sunrise in *Good Morning, Granny Rose* is followed quickly by a blizzard, mirroring the experience of the Luthers in *Where the Lilies Bloom*, who are beset by terrible cold spells and snow piled so deep that it brings down the roof of their shack. In *A Certain Small Shepherd*, Rebecca Caudill uses a blizzard as the central plot complication, and though it leads directly to a resolution of one character's handicap, it is nonetheless a truly life-threatening storm. Appalachia is a world of black snakes and rattlers, of hornets that can kill, of quick floods, of black bears. And yet, it is these elements of the myth that emphasize the beauty of the world. It is a hard beauty; no soft, zephyr-touched arcadia here. Beneath the beauty of the mountains lies the coming of winter and the knowledge that the mountains may be familiar, but are yet changeable. In children's literature, this knowledge drives many of the plot situations.

A second element of the myth of Appalachia is that life is lived in close proximity to the natural world. That world influences one's thought and feelings and understandings. In Gloria Houston's *The Year of the Perfect Christmas Tree* the splendor of the setting is conveyed principally through Barbara Cooney's illustrations. Here the valley of Pine Grove is bordered by craggy, rounded mountains, and their blue spruce collars merge into the many-hued blues of the sky. It is a green, gentle world, with pink sarvice trees in bloom and balsam growing "up high, near to heaven."[3] Pine Grove valley becomes a metaphor for the security of the family; when Ruthie's father leaves to fight in World War I, he is leaving the security of the family and of the valley itself. But when he returns, he comes back to both.

Time and again, books set in Appalachia stress this element. Lois Lenski's *Blue Ridge Billy* set in North Carolina, begins with Billy's awe at the beauty of the world about him: "The sun was setting. It threw a rosy glow over the mountains, that soft radiance that comes only between sundown and dark."[4] In Virginia Hamilton's *M.C. Higgins, the Great*, we first meet Higgins giving a ritualistic greeting to the sun rising over the Tennessee mountains. In *Where the Lilies Bloom*, the Luther children begin to earn money by wildcrafting, the gathering of medicinal roots and herbs. In Rebecca Caudill's *A Pocketful of Cricket*, Jay wanders through his farm knocking down hickory nuts, watching the nodding heads of the wildflowers, wading through the creek and almost stepping upon a crayfish, and picking a russet apple. And in Ruth Sawyer's *Journey Cake, Ho!*, the narrator notes that the world of the characters lies very close about them.

This natural world is not an isolating one, and a third strong element of the Appalachian myth is that for good or ill, life is lived in community, whether that community be defined as a family or a set of neighbors or even a small town. Sometimes this is suggested by the very form of the book, as in Richard Chase's *Jack Tales* and *Grandfather Tales* whose orality suggest that an audience has gathered to listen to the tales. (Chase dedicates his *Grandfather Tales* to those who discover that "No, it'll not do just to read the old tales out of a book. You've got to tell 'em to make 'em go right."[5]) And Cynthia Rylant's *Miss Maggie* begins with the affirmation that "what he [Nat] finally found is a story worth telling."[6] The sense here is that a community is being brought together by the tale, and that the telling is necessarily meant to be a communal event.

This sense of community also controls many of the plot situations in works set in Appalachia. In *Miss Maggie*, the young boy Nat must overcome his aversion to Miss Maggie before he can respond to her needs, and in so doing he discovers a friend instead of the storied hag he had imagined. In the end, he no longer listens to his feet, but only to his heart, as he finds that Miss Maggie has lost a beloved pet. His gift of a black snake named Henry is emblematic of a bonding between a child and an elderly person.

Several writers have used this element of the Appalachian myth to express the bonds that hold a family together. In *When I Was Young in the Mountains*, the closeness of the community, which gathers together to celebrate spiritual events, is mirrored by the closeness of the narrator's family. At times that family closeness can become so dominant that the family stands against the community, as in the Luther children's struggle to stay together in *Where the Lilies Bloom*, or in *The Year of the Perfect Christmas Tree*, where Ruthie and her mother's determination to find the perfect Christmas tree becomes an assertion of their *family-ness* in the face of the community's patronizing stance.

But other writers have used this same element of community to express the nature of tensions which arise within a family structure. In Doris Buchanan Smith's *Return to Bitter Creek*, set in North Carolina, the closeness of the extended family becomes the major source of conflict, as Lacey and her mother come under the scrutiny of Lacey's grandmother. The result is that Lacey's immediate family finds itself in conflict with the larger communal bonds, and the resolution of the novel becomes a resolution of these tensions. Similarly Katherine Paterson's *Come Sing, Jimmy Jo,* set in Virginia, explores the tensions that James feels as he begins to exercise "the gift." This leads to a breakup of his immediate family which James learns to deal with only as he redefines—and as the reader redefines—the meaning of family.

These same kinds of tensions are explored in two recent novels set in Appalachia. Carolyn Reeder's *Grandpa's Mountain* is set in Virginia's Blue Ridge mountains during the Depression; the government is acquiring land to establish the Shenandoah National Park. Carrie has come to visit her grandfather, who finds that his land is about to be condemned. When he tries to rally his neighbors to fight the government, he finds something most astonishing: his community is not with him. Faced with the possibilities of new homes with modern conveniences and good schools, most of the other families opt to sell their land to the government; Carrie's grandfather is thus left to fight for a community that has deserted him.

In Laurence Yep's *The Star Fisher* the community is pitted even more starkly against the individual family. Yep is best known for his exploration of the Chinese American experience, which is principally an experience of exclusion. That is the case here as well, as Joan and her family arrive in West Virginia in 1927 to establish a laundry and a new way of life. Joan's parents face the struggles of adapting to an American way of life; her mother especially sees their Chinese heritage seeping away, and tries desperately to hold onto it. But their greatest struggle is with a community not anxious to accept them.

Ruth White's *Sweet Creek Holler* shows the potential dangers of living in such close community. Set in Virginia, this autobiographical novel depicts the tensions that Ginny must face as her family moves to Sweet Creek Holler after their father has been murdered. Over and over again a rumor, perpetrated by neighbors, threatens to devastate her family. Her mother must prove that Ginny's father was not shot while stealing tires. And Ginny must face down innuendoes that a neighbor has abused her. Lou Jean, a beloved friend, does not have Ginny's strength; when she becomes pregnant and faces the scorn of her neighbors, she is driven to tragedy. The novel is a strong indictment of this element of Appalachian life, so that one can hardly hear the ripples of the sweet water for the pain of the author's childhood memories.

Perhaps the dominant element in the Appalachian myth is an unalloyed joy in the simple, in those things which lie close about us. In *Come Sing, Jimmy Jo*, James' mother and uncle are condemned as much for their rejection of this value as for their damage to the family. A sunrise in *Good Morning, Granny Rose*, the chirp of a cricket in *A Pocketful of Cricket*, the good dogs running the mountains in *Appalachia: The Voices of Sleeping Birds*, a walk along a road in *Return to Bitter Creek*, a common garden snake in *Miss Maggie*, a sunset in *Blue Ridge Billy*—all are simple elements which take on enormous meaning in these books, suggesting that joy is sometimes found in simplicity. Perhaps that is why the suggestion that Mary Call might one day have her own office and be a "big shot" is so unappealing and why Lacey's entrance into the community of Bitter Creek is so significant.

This joy in the simple is captured poignantly in Robert Burch's *Ida Early Comes Over the Mountain*. Ida comes to work for and live with a family of four children who have just lost their mother. She is remarkable for her unaffectedness, her refusal to accept conventional behavior, her child-like-ness, her delight in things like tid-dley-winks and milking and good desserts. This simplicity is also what leaves her open to deep hurt, the major crisis of the novel.

From *Appalachia: The Voices of Sleeping Birds* by Cynthia Rylant, illustrated by Barry Moser. Illustrations Copyright © 1991 by Penroyal Press, Inc. Reprinted by permission of Harcourt Brace Jovanovich, Inc.

In children's literature, this myth of Appalachia has been followed with remarkable consistency, and over and over again the elements of the myth come together to suggest that this is a world which is beautiful and eventful and close and simple and filled with every conceivable potential for adventure. It is, in short, a wonderful place to grow, "muddy and rolling," as Cynthia Rylant writes in *Waiting to Waltz*.[7] It is a world of contrasts, of warm and green valleys and killing blizzards, of individuality and the importance of community, of bounty and poverty. And yet, in some measure it is those very contrasts which help to make the world of Appalachia as it is pictured in children's literature so appealing.

At the end of *When I Was Young in the Mountains*, the narrator says that "When I was young in the mountains, I never wanted to go to the ocean, and I never wanted to go to the desert. I never wanted to go anywhere else in the world, for I was in the mountains. And that was always enough."[8]   The accompanying illustration shows her on the stoop of the cabin, holding a book and marking a place with her finger. Her eyes are looking away, out across the valley, and the smile that graces her face is one of complete contentment. It is a world where things are "enough," and therein lies its beauty and its potential for myth.

NOTES:

1. Cleaver, *Where the Lilies Bloom*, 8.

2. Ibid., 8.

3. Houston, *Year of the Perfect Christmas Tree.*

4. Lenski, *Blue Ridge Billy,* 1–2.

5. Chase, *Grandfather Tales.*

6. Rylant, *Miss Maggie.*

7. Rylant, *Waiting to Waltz,* 7.

8. Rylant, *When I Was Young in the Mountains.*

WORKS CITED:

Burch, Robert. *Ida Early Comes Over the Mountain.* New York: Viking, 1980.

Caudill, Rebecca. *A Certain Small Shepherd.* New York: Holt, 1965.

Caudill, Rebecca. *A Pocketful of Cricket.* New York: Holt, 1964.

Chase, Richard. *Grandfather Tales.* Boston, MA: Houghton Mifflin, 1948.

Chase, Richard. *Jack Tales.* Boston, MA: Houghton Mifflin, 1945.

Cleaver, Vera and Bill Cleaver. *Where the Lilies Bloom.* Philadelphia: J. B. Lippincott, 1969.

Hamilton, Virginia. *M. C. Higgins, the Great*. New York: Macmillan, 1974.

Houston, Gloria. *The Year of the Perfect Christmas Tree*. Illustrated by Barbara Cooney. New York: Dial, 1988.

Lenski, Lois. *Blue Ridge Billy*. New York: Dell, 1946.

Ludwig, Warren. *Good Morning, Granny Rose*. New York: Dutton, 1982.

Paterson, Katherine. *Come Sing, Jimmy Jo*. New York: Dutton, 1985.

Reeder, Carolyn. *Grandpa's Mountain*. New York: Macmillan, 1991.

Rylant, Cynthia. *Miss Maggie*. New York: Dutton, 1983.

Rylant, Cynthia. *Waiting to Waltz*. New York: Bradbury, 1984.

Rylant, Cynthia. *When I Was Young in the Mountains*. Illustrated by Diane Goode. New York: Dutton, 1982.

Sawyer, Ruth. *Journey Cake, Ho!* New York: Viking, 1953.

Smith, Doris Buchanan. *Return to Bitter Creek*. New York: Viking, 1986.

White, Ruth. *Sweet Creek Holler*. New York: Farrar, Straus, and Giroux, 1988.

Yep, Laurence. *The Star Fisher*. New York: Morrow, 1991.

BOOKS BY GARY SCHMIDT:

Hugh Lofting. New York: Macmillan, 1992.

Robert McClosky. New York: Twayne, 1990.

Sitting at the Feet of the Past: Retelling the North American Folktale for Children. Co-editor with Donald R. Hettinga. Westport, CT: Greenwood Press, 1992.

The Voice of the Narrator in Children's Literature: Insights from Writers and Critics. Co-editor with Charlotte F. Otten. Westport, CT: Greenwood Press, 1989.

ABOUT THE AUTHOR

Gary Schmidt is chair of the English Department, Calvin College in Grand Rapids, Michigan. He teaches courses related to children's literature, medieval literature, and the history of the language.

7

LITERATURE IN THE PEDIATRIC SETTING
THE USE OF BOOKS TO HELP MEET THE EMOTIONAL AND COGNITIVE NEEDS OF CHRONICALLY ILL CHILDREN

BY MARCELLA F. ANDERSON

Chronically ill, frequently hospitalized children can be viewed by themselves and by others as comprising a unique culture group within our larger community. These children can become physically and psychologically separated from family, from friends, from normal growing experiences, from information needed for success in school and job, and from participation in and knowledge of the larger world. Voids in growth and development contribute to a child's sense of isolation and lowered self-esteem. To encourage, respect, and strengthen these young people is to give them a chance to be an integral part of society. Books can be powerful tools in accomplishing these goals.

Today in the United States, there are over two million children with chronic illnesses. More than half of these children spend a third to a half of the year in the hospital. With medical advances, these statistics increase yearly as children and families cope more often with a life-threatening chronic illness than with imminent death.

Starting from the premise that literature can make a difference in the lives of chronically ill, hospitalized children, let us consider how books and stories can help in two specific areas: *cognitive growth* and *emotional development*.

INFANTS AND TODDLERS
0– 30 MONTHS

Cognitive: Very young children need to hear the sounds of language, particularly rhythm, repetition, and sometimes rhyme. Too often in pediatric settings this age child hears only footsteps in the hall, fragmented speech, and the continuous beeping of medical equipment. Nursery rhymes and hand play like Patty-Cake and others like those found in *Hand Rhymes* (Brown) can give the child an enriched environment for learning language.

Sometimes under stress of hospitalization and separation from the familiar, this age child will end her early efforts at verbal communication. Interactive books, such as *Where's Spot?* (Hill) encourage early efforts to talk. Other books depicting familiar activities like *All Fall Down* (Oxenbury) and familiar objects like *What's This?* (Hoban) help this age child to feel freed into "talking" again.

Emotional: Separation from the parent is a major trauma for this age child. Because the child, however young, will recognize a parent's voice, parents should be encouraged to read aloud to their hospitalized children. Sometimes parents can make a tape of themselves reading aloud. In their absence, this tape can be played by other caregivers. *Goodnight Moon* (Brown) and *The Little Chick* (McCue) are good choices.

PRESCHOOLERS
30 MONTHS – 5 YEARS

Cognitive: Learning about the world is important for the preschooler. The chronically ill, hospitalized child this age may be confined to his bed and see only tall buildings out his of window. To help the child learn about the world outside the hospital, try reading *The Listening Walk* (Showers) and *Harry, the Dirty Dog* (Zion). *Wake Up, Farm* (Tressalt) and *The Biggest Truck* (Lyons) introduce the child to jobs and settings other than hospital workers and health environments. *Bear Child's Book of Special Days*

(Rockwell) and *My Spring Robin* (Rockwell) help the child to experience the richness of the passing year.

Preschoolers not stimulated in the hospital environment lose precious opportunities to develop imagination—and so, also lack the capacity to escape into fantasy from the hospital experience. *Pretend You're a Cat* (Marzollo) and *It's Just Me, Emily* (Hines) can awaken the young child's imagination.

Emotional: Preschoolers also fear separation from parents and are reassured by books like *Runaway Bunny* (Brown) and *Whose Mouse Are You?* (Kraus).

This age child worries too about losing recently acquired skills and general competence, and so delights in *Whistle for Willie* (Keats), *How Do I Put It On?* (Watanabe), *Anna in Charge* (Tsutsui), and *Swimmy* (Lionni).

SCHOOL-AGE CHILDREN
6 – 12

Cognitive: Children this age need and want information. The chronically ill, hospitalized child should have access to information too through histories like *Now Is Your Time* (Myers) and *The Wright Brothers: How They Invented the Airplane* (Freedman). Sharks and dinosaurs are favorite subjects, as are general topics such as undersea exploration, physics, astronomy, and the human body.

Reading while hospitalized can help develop a sense of values and introduce skills involved in making choices. Recommended titles are *On My Honor* (Bauer), *Shiloh* (Naylor), and *Song of the Trees* (Taylor).

Parents are often overwhelmed by their child's life-threatening diagnosis and focus all their energies on the child's illness, meanwhile failing to prepare him for ordinary life transitions, such as starting school in its various stages. This child can become acquainted with these experiences through books like *When Will I Read?* (Cohen) and *Nothing's Fair in Fifth Grade* (DeClements).

Strider (Cleary) and *Are You There, God? It's Me, Margaret* (Blume) can support the child entering adolescence.

Emotional: This age child seeks personal accomplishment and independence, both difficult goals to achieve when chronically ill and hospitalized. Survival stories such as *The Sign of the Beaver* (Speare) and *Island of the Blue Dolphins* (O'Dell) and stories of heroism like *Number the Stars* (Lowry) and *St. George and The Dragon* (Hodges) can inspire and be lived vicariously. Sometimes, simply a steady day-to-day coping as in *The Long Winter* (Wilder), *M. C. Higgins, the Great* (Hamilton) and *Homecoming* (Voigt) can be supportive and uplifting in itself.

The chronically ill, hospitalized school-age child misses greatly the companionship of his or her peers. Isolated, this child can quite naturally imagine that they are alone in their feelings and concerns. Reading books like those their contemporaries are reading can reassure them that others share their thoughts and feelings. *Anastasia Krupnik* (Lowry) and *Wanted: Mud Blossom* (Byars) are titles in warm and often amusing family series with easily identifiable main characters. *The Secret Garden* (Burnett) and *The Black Stallion* (Farley) are classics that still appeal to and affirm the school-age child.

HUMOR AND QUIETNESS

Across all age groups of chronically ill, hospitalized children, books with humor and quietness offer their own support and solace. Books that help the children laugh and feel calm and reassured promote stress reduction and the release of natural pain blockers called endorphins. Frequently, a sense of well-being ensues, providing an opportunity for healing to begin.

A few popular, humorous titles are *I Took My Frog to the Library* (Kimmel), *The Stupids Step Out* (Allard), *Ramona and Her Father* (Cleary), and *The B.F.G.* (Dahl).

A quiet serenity and beauty can be found in *Sailing With the Wind* (Locker), *The Lost Lake* (Say) and *Sarah, Plain and Tall*

(MacLachlan). A particularly lovely book written in prose poetry and sensitively illustrated is *Owl Moon* (Yolen). A terminally ill child asked his foster mother for a copy of *Owl Moon* from the hospital library. His mother read the book several times to him before the child died.

CONCLUSION

Today, fast moving medical advances are leading the way to fuller and longer lives for many children with chronic illnesses. There is more emphasis on social and psychological support and reintegration into the larger community. With the firm belief that chronically ill, hospitalized young patients are children first, we can use books to enable and empower them to become enriching participants in a multicultural society.

WORKS CITED

Allard, Harry. *The Stupids Step Out*. Ill. by James Marshall. Boston: Houghton Mifflin, 1974.

Bauer, Marion Dale. *On My Honor*. New York: Clarion, 1986.

Blume, Judy. *Are You There, God? It's Me, Margaret*. New York: Bradbury, 1970.

Brown, Marc Tolon. *Hand Rhymes*. New York: Dutton, 1985.

Brown, Margaret Wise. *Goodnight Moon*. New York: Harper, 1947.

———. *Runaway Bunny.* Ill. by Clement Hurd. New York: Harper Collins, 1991.

Burnett, Frances Hodgson. *The Secret Garden*. Ill. by Tasha Tudor. Philadelphia: Lippincott, 1962.

Byars, Betsy. *Wanted: Mud Blossom*. Ill. by Jacqueline Rogers. New York: Delacorte, 1991.

Cleary, Beverly. *Ramona and Her Father*. Ill. by Alan Tiegreen. New York: Morrow, 1977.

———. *Strider*. Ill. by Paul O. Zelinsky. New York: Morrow, 1991.

Cohen, Miriam. *When Will I Read?* Ill. by William Hoban. New York: Greenwillow, 1977.

Dahl, Roald. *The B.F.G.* Ill. by Quentin Blake. New York: Farrar, Straus, Giroux, 1982.

DeClements, Barthe. *Nothing's Fair in Fifth Grade*. New York: Viking, 1981.

Faily, Walter. *The Black Stallion*. New York: Scholastic, 1979.

Freedman, Russell. *The Wright Brothers: How They Invented the Airplane*. New York: Holiday House, 1991.

Hamilton, Virginia. *M. C. Higgins, the Great*. New York: Dell, 1974.

Hill, Eric. *Where's Spot*. New York: Putnam, 1980.

Hines, Anna Grossnickle. *It's Just Me, Emily*. New York: Clarion, 1987.

Hoban, Tana. *What is it?* New York: Greenwillow, 1985.

Hodges, Margaret. *Saint George and the Dragon: A Golden Legend*. Ill. by Trina Schart Hyma. Boston: Little Brown, 1984.

Keats, Ezra Jack. *Whistle for Willie*. New York: Viking, 1964.

Kimmel, Eric. *I Took My Frog to the Library*. Ill. by Blanche Sims. New York: Viking Penguin, 1990.

Kraus, Robert. *Whose Mouse Are You?* Ill. by Jose Aruego. New York: Macmillan, 1970.

Lionni, Leo. *Swimmy*. New York: Pantheon, 1968.

Locker, Thomas. *Sailing With the Wind*. New York: Dial, 1986.

Lowry, Lois. *Anastasia Krupnik*. Boston: Houghton Mifflin, 1979.

———. *Number the Stars*. Boston: Houghton Mifflin, 1989.

Lyons, David. *The Biggest Truck.* New York: Lothrop, 1988.

McCue, Lisa. *The Little Chick.* New York: Random House, 1986.

MacLachlan, Patricia. *Sarah, Plain and Tall.* New York: Harper & Row, 1985.

Marzollo, Jean. *Pretend You're a Cat.* Ill. by Jerry Pinkney. New York: Dial, 1990.

Myers, Walter Dean. *Now is Your Time: The African-American Struggle for Freedom.* New York: HarperCollins, 1991.

Naylor, Phyllis Reynolds. *Shiloh.* New York: Atheneum, 1991.

O'Dell, Scott. *Island of the Blue Dolphins.* New York: Dell, 1960.

Oxenbury, Helen. *All Fall Down.* New York: Alladin, 1987.

Rockwell, Anne. *Bear Child's Book of Special Days.* New York: Dutton, 1989.

———. *My Spring Robin.* Ill. by Harlow & Lizzy Rockwell. New York: Macmillan, 1989.

Say, Allen. *The Lost Lake.* Boston: Houghton Mifflin, 1989.

Showers, Paul. *The Listening Walk.* Ill. by Aliki Hayashi. New York: Crowell, 1961.

Speare, Elizabeth George. *The Sign of the Beaver.* Boston: Houghton Mifflin, 1983.

Taylor, Mildred D. *Song of the Trees.* Ill. by Jerry Pinkney. New York: Dial, 1975.

Tressalt, Alvin. *Wake Up, Farm!* Ill. by Carolyn Ewing. New York: Lothrop, Lee & Shepard, 1991.

Tsutsui, Yoriko. *Anna in Charge.* Ill. by Akiki Hayashi. New York: Puffin, 1991.

Voigt, Cynthia. *Homecoming.* New York: Atheneum, 1981.

Watanabe, Shigeo. *How Do I Put It On?* Ill. by Yasuo Ohtomo. New York: Collins, 1979.

Wilder, Laura Ingalls. *The Long Winter*. Ill. by Garth Williams. New York: Harper & Row, 1971.

Yolen, Jane. *Owl Moon*. Ill. by John Schoenherr. New York: Philomel, 1987.

Zion, Gene. *Harry, The Dirty Dog*. Ill. by Margaret Bloy Graham. New York: Harper & Row, 1956.

BOOKS BY
MARCELLA F. ANDERSON:

Books and Children in Pediatric Settings: A Guide for Caregivers and Librarians. Cleveland, OH: Rainbow Babies and Children's Hospital, 1988.

ABOUT THE AUTHOR

Marcella F. Anderson is the Patient / Family Librarian, Rainbow Babies and Children's Hospital, Cleveland, Ohio.

8

JEWISH AMERICAN EXPERIENCES IN CHILDREN'S BOOKS

BY ESTHER COHEN HEXTER

A man came to the Priest [of the Temple] Shammai and asked Shammai to teach him "the whole Torah" [all of Jewish law] while he stood on one foot. Shammai laughed, said it was impossible and sent him away. So the man went to Shammai's rival the great Rabbi Hillel and asked him to teach him the whole Torah while he stood on one foot. And Hillel replied, "What is hateful to you, do not to your neighbor: that is the whole Torah, while the rest is commentary thereof; go and learn it."

Talmud, Shabbat 31a[1]

INTRODUCTION

The inclusion of the study of Judaism and the Jewish experience has its rightful place in any classroom or library which seeks to examine the various cultural/religious groups that make up the United States. From 1654 when the first Jews set foot in New Amsterdam (now New York) until today, Jews and the Jewish tradition have made significant contributions to the fabric of American society.

The body of literature on Judaism and the Jewish experience is varied and extensive, especially on the adult level. In my years as director of a teacher/community resource center and as librarian for a synagogue library, I have seen a major change in quality and quantity of Jewish children's books published. Not that many years ago, many of the books were restricted, relatively routine stories showing children observing Jewish holidays or a retelling of familiar Bible stories. Illustrations were rarely colorful or lively. Most of the books were published by small Jewish publishing houses. Fortunately this has changed. Every year brings a greater variety and higher quality of stories, beautifully illustrated, by a growing number of authors. Many of these books now are published by general or "trade" publishers.[2] There is a greater effort to find, translate, and write down, in a form suitable for children to read or adults to tell orally, many of the rabbinic legends and popular folktales.

Judaism is in itself a multicultural tradition. It has a number of denominations and many different religious expressions. Jews today and through the ages have developed and spoken a number of different Jewish languages, each with its own literary tradition. These include Hebrew, Yiddish (Judeo-German), and Ladino (Judeo-Spanish) to name a few. Jews have lived all over the world, adapting and adopting customs from these many lands of residence to blend with and enrich the Jewish tradition.

Judaism is at the same time a religion, a culture, a people, and a nation. With this in mind, I would like to share some brief thoughts on what Judaism and the Jewish experience is all about. It is my hope that this will aide librarians and teachers in selecting materials for their students.

As an introduction, one needs to understand the basic tenants of Judaism. These basics are and have been subject to a variety of interpretations by different schools of thought and different branches of Judaism. Briefly, Jews believe in Adonoi Ehad, One God. This belief has been called ethical monotheism. The Jewish religion is based on Torah, its revealed scripture. In the narrow sense Torah is The Five Books of Moses, the first five books of the Bible, which contain the laws that form the basis of Jewish life. Torah also relates the stories of the fathers and mothers of the Jewish people and their encounter with God. In the broader sense Torah is the entire Hebrew Bible.

The basic tenants of Judaism also include a belief in Am Yisrael, the people Israel, or Jewish peoplehood; and Eretz Yisrael,

JEWISH AMERICAN EXPERIENCES

the Land of Israel, the Land promised by God to Abraham and his descendants. Though there is much diversity, Jews all share a common language, Hebrew, the language of Torah, the Bible, and prayer. In this modern world Hebrew has again become a spoken language, in Israel and beyond, with a rich secular literature of its own.

Religious commentary and interpretation of Jewish law written by scholars seek to clarify and explain the relationship of God to the Jewish people and the people's relationship to God. These scholars, often rabbis which means "teacher," seek to explain the laws set down in Torah and Talmud (see Note 1), which form guiding principles for life. Finally, Jews have also developed a rich folklore and story telling tradition to add joy as well as an understanding of what it means to be a Jew.

Clearly to gain insight into Judaism and the Jewish experience, or any culture's experience, a person has to view it through the eyes of those who know it well; otherwise the picture becomes distorted. In seeking to better understand the Jewish experience, the librarian or teacher needs to keep in mind the common religious root, the Hebrew Bible, of Judaism and Christianity (and Islam). Very often in the United States, where Christianity is the religion of the majority, many people assume the Christian interpretation of stories, customs or events from the Hebrew Bible, which Christians call the Old Testament, to be the only valid ones.

Let me illustrate with a story. The recreation director of the nursing home where my father lives said she wanted to share the Hanukah story and some of its customs with the residents. At her request I provided a simple, clear, and accurate account of the story and its significance for Jews and Judaism. In truth, Hanukah is a relatively minor festival in the Jewish religious cycle. I stressed its major importance was that Hanukah was the first holiday that celebrates the struggle for religious freedom. I was unable to be there for the beginning of the Hanukah party. When I walked in, a colleague of the recreation director, was telling the story of Hanukah, from Maccabees I, the textual source. Unfortunately she had ignored the Jewish source material and interpretations of text I had provided. I was shocked to hear her giving a Christian interpretation to the Jewish Festival of Freedom. Surely studying the Book of Maccabees from a Christian viewpoint has validity, but not when describing the significance of the Jewish festival of Hanukah.

GENERAL INFORMATION AND RESOURCES

I mention all of the above as a caution to anyone who has the responsibility to select books on Judaism for teachers or students. In preparing this chapter on Jewish American literary experiences, I was guided by the following principles. For public schools, I feel it most appropriate to select books on Judaism as a culture, books about the different parts of the Jewish people, or books that describe the Jewish religion and its beliefs. I would not recommend selecting books that seek to instruct one on how to act, live or think as a Jew. For example, I have omitted books of Bible stories or rabbinic wisdom literature, which I would include on a bibliography for a Jewish religious school.

I have prepared a selected annotated bibliography of children's literature on four different levels: primary; upper elementary; middle school; and high school. In making my recommendations, I tried to consider limited resources. The books chosen represent works on holidays, customs, and ceremonies, what Jews believe, life cycle events, Jews around the world, the American Jewish experience, Holocaust and Israel. A number of nonfiction works are included, because of the need to "cover" the many different aspects of the Jewish experience. Were I to write a follow-up piece, I would concentrate more on fiction and biography. I considered Jewish themes as well as Jewish writers. In this chapter, I am presenting the books by theme and topic, not by age grouping.

Any list of great children's writers should include, but not be limited to, Sydney Taylor, Barbara Cohen, Marilyn Hirsh, Malka Drucker, Miriam Chaikin. This list is growing yearly, and is partially responsible for the explosion of children's books on Jewish themes in recent years.³ Works for children by Isaac Bashevis Singer should find their way into any selection. Singer, a Nobel Laureate in Literature (Yiddish) in 1978, is a master storyteller in the tradition of the oral storytellers from Eastern European Jewish tradition. All of his works were written in Yiddish and translated into English. Many of his short stories are wonderful read or told orally.

For older students or any teacher the list of great writers is a long one. One of course must be selective. I include this list of writers for those who already have a good basic collection. For middle and high school students one must add works by Milton Meltzer, a superb and highly readable social historian. For teens and adults choose from the fiction of Saul Bellow (a Nobel Laureate in Literature [United States] 1976), Chaim Potok, Bernard Malamud, Cynthia Ozik, Anzia Yeizerska, Philip Roth, Tillie Olsen, Leon Uris, and of course, Isaac Bashevis Singer. One cannot miss including at least something of 1986 Nobel Peace Prize Winner and outstanding spokesman on the Holocaust, Elie Wiesel. For someone who wants to understand the Eastern European Jewish experience and enjoy outstanding writing and humor, consider the works of Yiddish writer Sholom Aleichem, all translated into English.

Before discussing some of the specific books, here are some general resources. The Jewish Book Council publishes *Jewish Book World* quarterly and *The Selected Children's Judaica Collection*; sponsors Jewish Book Month; and gives National Jewish Book Awards.⁴ The Association of Jewish Libraries, presents children's book awards annually; and prepares selected bibliographies.⁵

Jewish Publication Society of America (J.P.S.) is an outstanding publisher of all types of Judaica (children's-adult).⁶ Kar-Ben Copies, Inc. has superb books for primary graders.⁷ J.P.S. and Lodestar (Dutton) have wonderful Jewish biography series for upper elementary or middle school students. Marcia Posner, Ph.D., a past President of Association of Jewish Libraries, has written *Jewish Children's Books: How to Choose Them, How to Use Them*. She also has articles on children's literature in the *Encyclopedia Judaica* and in its *1983/85 Year Book*.

Finally, the United States Congress has set aside one week every spring in April or May as National Jewish Heritage Week to celebrate Jewish culture and the contributions of Jews to the United States.[8]

SELECTED WORKS

To enter the world of the Jewish experience, perhaps the best portal is through Shabbat (the Sabbath). Shabbat is a day of rest, prayer and family togetherness that occurs every week.

With the words, "Shabbat is coming! Shabbat is coming soon! " Faige Kobre in *A Sense of Shabbat*, takes young readers on a journey into the warmth, peace, and love that families celebrating Shabbat can feel.

The Hanukah Story by Marilyn Hirsh retells the story of the fight for religious freedom and how this led to the modern holiday celebration. Hirsh's research into types of clothing and armor lend much to the illustrations and to her spirited telling of the tale. In *All About Hanukah*, Judye Groner and Madeline Wikler explore, among other themes, what it feels like to be a Jewish child in America in December. With this in mind, teachers need to discuss the Jewish experience at times other than Hanukah and use other holidays as illustration. One delightful way to do this is to introduce children to *The Carp in the Bathtub* by Barbara Cohen, a wonderful story for Passover fun reading, or any time.

Jewish folklore forms part of the core of the story telling tradition. I have selected two examples from the Eastern European Yiddish tradition. Scholars and storytellers are currently exploring the folk traditions of communities of the Jewish people from the Middle East, North Africa and beyond. It is fairly safe to predict that the fruit of their efforts will make its way into juvenile Judaica before too long.

Uri Shulevitz certainly deserves the Caldecott Honor Award he received for *The Treasure*. Through his richly colored paintings, you can really sense the powerful pull of Isaac's journey through forests and over mountains to find his treasure.

Margot Zemach explores the age old tradition of turning to the rabbi to help solve problems in *It Could Always Be Worse*. "'Holy rabbi,' he cried, 'things are in a bad way with me and getting worse. We are so poor that my mother, my wife, my six children, and I all live together in one small hut. We are too crowded, and there's so much noise. Help me, Rabbi. I'll do whatever you say,'" You and your readers will laugh at Zemach's funny drawings and the rabbi's solution. Maybe you will even see parallels in your own or other traditions.

Jewish juvenile literature published in the United States often explores what it is like to make the transition from the "Old World" to a new life in America. "I heard Elizabeth laugh out loud. 'My goodness Molly,' she cried. 'That's not a Pilgrim. That's some Russian or Polish person.'" This is the critical scene in award winning author Barbara Cohen's *Molly's Pilgrim*. This wonderful book has been made into a movie and also makes a delightful dramatization for children. Try it at Thanksgiving time for a different view of giving thanks for being in the United States. Sydney Taylor also explores immigrant life by taking his *All-of-a-Kind Family* all over town in his highly popular five-book series. They have been reprinted many times over the years.

These books are all relatively recent. The best book on the immigrant transition, which hundreds of thousands of Jews made in coming to the United States, was written between 1898 and 1902 by Hutchins Hapgood. Hapgood, was given the assignment as a journalist to try to capture *The Spirit of the Ghetto: Studies of the Jewish Quarter of New York*. He did so in this highly readable classic illustrated by the then unknown young artist, Jacob Epstein. Teens could easily be captivated by his walks down dark hallways into crowded tenement apartments teeming with confusion of trying to make it in the new world while holding onto something of the old.

I highly recommend two novels to complete this introduction to the Jewish American immigrant experience. *Bread Givers* by Anzia Yezierska gives us a compelling view of conflict between father and daughter, as she desperately works at breaking out of the poverty of tenement life. This work is unique in its genre, as it is actually an early feminist novel. Henry Roth gives a magnificent view of the immigrant experience from the eyes of a young boy coming of age in *Call It Sleep*. Roth is a master at using the broken English of the newest Americans of their day in dialogue on the street, while using proper English to connote when they are speaking Yiddish at home to each other.

But Jews are not all from Eastern Europe and all Jewish American literary experiences do not take place at the turn of the century. A most stirring journey "home" to Israel has been made recently by the ancient community of Jews of Ethiopia. Aided greatly by the powerful, but simple black and white drawings of illustrator Alemu Eshetie, himself an Ethiopian immigrant of a few years ago, Jonathan Kendall tells the moving story of their proud heritage in *My Name Is Rachamim*. Mira Meir in her book *Alina: A Russian Girl Comes to Israel*, traces another "homecoming." This is an excellent story for understanding how to treat any newcomer. It also celebrates the major immigration of former Soviet Jews to Israel.

Norman Finkelstein's *The Other 1492: Jewish Settlement in the New World*, is a compelling book about the Spanish Jews (also known as Sepharadim), their great contribution to Spanish and Jewish culture before being expelled from Spain in 1492, and their "rebirth" in the Americas. There

From *My Name is Rachamim* by Jonathan P. Kendall. Illustrated by Alemu Eshetie. Copyright © 1987 by Union of American Hebrew Congregations

will be other books about the Sepharadim as Jewish Americans reflect on the "other 1492," a sad chapter in Jewish history.

No discussion about Jewish American juvenile literature would be complete without some mention of exceptional books on the Holocaust. In *Number the Stars*, the 1990 Newbery Award winner by Lois Lowry, we have a sensitively written novel based on fact about the rescue of Danish Jews by their countrymen. Bea Stadtler's *The Holocaust: A History of Courage and Resistance*, remains an important work and would make an excellent text for middle school students. *Night*, by Elie Wiesel and *All But My Life*, by Gerda Klein are two outstanding autobiographies by Holocaust survivors.

In general, it is my recommendation to use historical, documentary, or eyewitness accounts when teaching about the Holocaust. It is too easy for a poorly written novel to support claims of revisionists either that the Holocaust, destruction of much of European Jewry and millions of other innocents, never happened or that its death toll has been greatly exaggerated. I would also caution teachers not to start discussing this difficult topic too early. From my years in the classroom and in advising teachers on Holocaust resources, my suggestion would be to save this reading and exploration for middle school years and beyond.

From *Number the Stars* by Lois Lowry. Copyright © 1989 by Lois Lowry. Reprinted by permission of Houghton Mifflin Co. All rights reserved.

In keeping with Jewish tradition followed when one studies a selection from the Torah, I will end on a more hopeful note. The Jewish American literary offerings include numerous biographies on such individuals as Emma Lazarus, who wrote the famous sonnet on the Statue of Liberty; and Haym Salomon, a little known hero of the American Revolution.[9] For others consult the Lodestar (Dutton) or J.P.S. Jewish biography series cited above.

I will leave you with the aura of *My Special Friend*, by Floreva G. Cohen. Better than my own comments, here are the words of Jesse Nurick excerpted from his entry in a writing contest. His topic is a favorite book he has read.

> This book is about a boy with Down's Syndrome, just like me. He has a friend who helps him study Torah. I have a brother who helps me study Torah.... He is proud to be a young Jewish man. So am I! He helps his friend sometimes, and other times, his friend helps him.[10]

What better thought on which to end this chapter. If we are to grow ourselves and help young people grow to a greater appreciation of the cultural diversity which makes our country great, we have much to learn from Jesse Nurick and from Cohen's sensitive and beautiful book.

It is my hope that the works cited and suggestions made will encourage teachers and librarians who do not presently include works of literature about the Jewish experience in their collections/curricula to do so.

NOTES:

1. Talmud is a compilation of rabbinic discussions of explanations of the Laws in the Torah (Five Books of Moses). Together with Torah it forms the basis of Jewish law and life. This legend seems particularly appropriate when one is trying to condense a difficult topic into a few words.

2. Posner, Marcia, *Jewish Children's Books*, 5.

3. Marcia Posner's "Jewish Juvenile Books" article in *Jewish Book Annual*, lists on average over 60 new children's books of Jewish content published in America each year. *Jewish Book World*, 30.

4. Jewish Book Council, 15 East 26th Street, New York, N.Y. 10010-1579, (212) 532-4949.

5. Association of Jewish Libraries, c/o National Foundation of Jewish Culture, 122 East 42nd Street, New York, N.Y. 10168, Rm. 1512.

6. Jewish Publication Society of America, 1930 Chestnut Street, Philadelphia, PA 19103-4599.

7. Kar-Ben Copies, Inc., 6800 Tildenwood Lane, Rockville, MD 20852.

8. Rabbi Mark H. Levine's *Celebrating Jewish Heritage Week: Lesson Plans for Kindergarten Through Sixth Grade*, provides five mini-biographies, complete with lesson plans for each grade. Order from Board of Jewish Education of Greater Washington, 11710 Hunters Lane, Rockville, MD 20852.

9. *I Lift My Lamp, Emma Lazarus and the Statue of Liberty*, by Nancy Smiler Levinson, Lodestar Books (E. P. Dutton), New York, 1986; and *Haym Salomon' Liberty's Son*, by Shirley Milgrim, Jewish Publication Service of America, Philadelphia, 1975.

10. This review received an award in the Shofar magazine/Jewish Book Council 1990 writing contest for children from grades 1-8. *Jewish Book World*, op. cit., 6.

WORKS CITED:

Cohen, Barbara, *Molly's Pilgrim*, illustrated by Michael Deraney, Bantam First Skylark Book, New York, 1990.

———, *The Carp in the Bathtub*, illustrated by Joan Halpern, Lothrop, Lee & Shepard Co., New York, 1972.

Cohen, Floreva G., *My Special Friend*, Board of Jewish Education of Greater New York, New York, 1989.

"Children's Literature" in *Encyclopaedia Judaica*, Volume 5, Keter Publishing House Jerusalem Ltd., Jerusalem, Israel, 1972, 428-460.

——— in *Encyclopaedia Judaica Year Book 1983/85*, 1985, 235-237.

Finkelstein, Norman, *The Other 1492: Jewish Settlement in the New World*, Charles Scribner's Sons, New York, 1989.

Groner, Judye and Madeline Wikler, *All About Hanukah*, illustrated by Rosalyn Schanzer, Kar-Ben Copies, Inc., Rockville, Maryland, 1988.

Hapgood, Hutchins, *Spirit of the Ghetto: Studies of the Jewish Quarter of New York*, drawings from life by Jacob Epstein, Harvard University Press, Cambridge, Massachusetts, 1967. (originally written 1904-1905)

Hirsh, Marilyn, *The Hanukah Story*, Bonim Books [A division of Hebrew Publishing Company], New York, 1977.

Jewish Book World, Spring 1991, Volume 9, No. 2, Jewish Book Council, New York.

Kendall, Jonathan P., *My Name Is Rachamim*, illustrated by Alemu Eshetie, Union of American Hebrew Congregations, New York, 1987.

Klein, Gerda, *All But My Life*, Noonday (Hill and Wang), New York, 1971.

Kobre, Faige, *A Sense of Shabbat*, Torah Aura Productions, Los Angeles, California, 1989.

Lowry, Lois, *Number the Stars*, Houghton Mifflin Company, Boston, 1990. 1990 Newbery Medal.

Meir, Mira, *Alina: A Russian Girl Comes to Israel*, Zeva Shapiro translator, Jewish Publication Society of America, Philadelphia, 1982.

Posner, Marcia, Ph.D., *Jewish Children's Books: How to Choose Them, How to Use Them*, Hadassah, 50 W. 58th Street, New York, N.Y. 10019, 1986.

Roth, Henry, *Call It Sleep*, Farrar, Straus & Giroux, New York, 1991. (originally written in 1934)

Shulevitz, Uri, *The Treasure*, Farrar, Straus & Giroux, New York, 1978. Caldecott Honor Book 1980.

Stadtler, Bea, *The Holocaust: A History of Courage and Resistance*, Behrman House, New York, 1974.

Taylor, Sydney, *All-of-a-Kind Family*, Taylor Productions, New York, 1988 (hb; reprint); Dell, New York, 1980 (pb).

Wiesel, Elie, *Night*, Bantam Books, New York, 1982. (original copyright Farrar Straus & Giroux, 1960)

Yezierska, Anzia, *Bread Givers: A Novel*, Persea Books, New York, 1975. (original copyright 1925)

Zemach, Margot, *It Could Always Be Worse*, Farrar Straus & Giroux, New York, 1990. Caldecott Honor Book 1977.

JEWISH AMERICAN LITERARY EXPERIENCES

ANNOTATED BIBLIOGRAPHY

Primary

Aronin, Ben, *The Secret of the Sabbath Fish*, pictures by Shay Rieger, Jewish Publication Society of America, Philadelphia, 1978.

> Retelling of Eastern European folktale of how gefilte fish came into being. In creating this Sabbath (holiday) delicacy, we learn what has happened to the Jewish people through the ages.

Bar-Nissim, Barbara, *The Jews: One People*, illustrated by Marlene Lobell Ruthen, United Synagogue of America Commission on Jewish Education, New York, 1989.

> Wonderful exploration of Jewish peoplehood; its many differences in custom, costume, architecture, but also strong unifying beliefs, holidays, life cycle events.

Cohen, Barbara, *Molly's Pilgrim*, illustrated by Michael Deraney, Bantam First Skylark Book, New York, 1990. (other editions available) [Author is winner of Sydney Taylor Body-of-Work Award, from Association of Jewish Libraries. Film version won Academy Award for Best Short Film in 1985.]

> Delightful story of family who moves to the U.S. from Russia in the early twentieth century to find freedom. Everyone has to bring a Pilgrim doll to school for Thanksgiving. Molly's doll, which looks like a Russian peasant, helps children learn the true meaning of the holiday. *This book is a must to teach tolerance for those of other cultures.*

———, *The Carp in the Bathtub*, illustrated by Joan Halpern, Lothrop, Lee & Shepard Co., New York, 1972. (many editions, including Dell Yearling)

> Barbara Cohen's story has become a modern classic tale for Passover. Children who love animal stories will sympathize with the characters in this book.

Costabel, Eva Deutsch, *The Jews of New Amsterdam*, Antheneum, New York, 1988.

> Tells the story of the first Jewish settlement in North America, with simple text and lovely pictures that show both the life of the Jews and of this early Dutch colony.

Gallant, Janet, *My Brother's Bar Mitzvah*, illustrated by Susan Avishai, Kar-Ben Copies, Inc., Rockville, Maryland, 1990.

> Sarah is worried that her big brother who still acts "like a child" will not be ready to become a Bar Mitzvah.

Groner, Judye and Madeline Wikler, *All About Hanukah*, illustrated by Rosalyn Schanzer, Kar-Ben Copies, Inc., Rockville, Maryland, 1988.

> Book includes an retelling of the Hanukah story, plus customs, ceremonies, recipes, games, and an important discussion of what it means to be "different," especially being a Jew in the United States in December. A good reference for teachers.

Harvey, Brett, *Immigrant Girl, Becky of Eldridge Street,* illustrated by Deborah Kogan Ray, Holiday House, New York, 1987.

> Becky and her family emigrated from Russia to avoid being persecuted because they were Jews. This book explores the excitement of growing up in New York City in 1910.

Hirsh, Marilyn, *The Hanukah Story*, Bonim Books [A division of Hebrew Publishing Company], New York, 1977.

> Retells the story of how Judah Maccabee and his small army won victory over Syrian/Greeks in ancient Israel and how this victory led to celebration of Hanukah. Hirsch's accuracy and *superb illustrations* make this one of the best books about the world's first victory for religious freedom.

Kobre, Faige, *A Sense of Shabbat*, Torah Aura Productions, Los Angeles, California, 1989.

> Photos and text take you to a child's view of getting ready for and celebrating Shabbat through the five senses. This book beautifully captures the "magic" of Shabbat (the Sabbath).

Meir, Mira, *Alina: A Russian Girl Comes to Israel*, Zeva Shapiro. translator, Jewish Publication Society of America, Philadelphia, 1982.

> Beautiful photos illustrate the frustrations and eventual joys of acclamation to a new home by a young "Russian" Jew. Excellent story for understanding how to treat any newcomer. Highlights the important "Russian Jewish" movement for religious freedom and "return" to their Jewish homeland.

Portnoy, Mindy Avra, *Ima On the Bima; My Mommy is a Rabbi*, illustrated by Stefi Karen Rubin, Kar-Ben Copies, Inc., Rockville, Maryland, 1986.

> Duties and activities of being a rabbi are described through the eyes of Rabbi Portnoy's daughter.

Rosen, Anne, Jonathan & Norma, *A Family Passover*, photography by Laurence Salzmann, Jewish Publication Society of American, Philadelphia, 1980.

> Story told by a ten-year-old girl of an actual family preparing for and celebrating this most special of Jewish holidays.

Shulevitz, Uri, *The Treasure*, Farrar, Straus and Giroux, New York, 1978. Caldecott Honor Book - 1980.

> Magnificently illustrated telling of the classic folk story of the man who follows his dream to a distant city to find treasure, only to be sent back to his own home to successfully complete his search.

Steiner, Connie Colker, *On Eagles Wings and Other Things*, Jewish Publication Society of America, Philadelphia, 1987.

> After World War II Jewish children leave Yemen, Tunisia, America, and Poland with their families to make Israel their new home. Book traces their lives, getting ready, and their long and varied journeys to gathering in the Jewish national homeland.

Zemach, Margot, *It Could Always Be Worse*, A Yiddish Folktale Retold with Pictures (by author), Farrar, Straus and Giroux, New York, 1990. Caldecott Honor Book - 1977.

Wonderful retelling of a classic Eastern European Jewish story. Shows how Jews of little towns depended on the rabbi for help. Illustrations capture not only the spirit of the tale, but also the spirit of daily life.

UPPER ELEMENTARY

Adler, David A., *Our Golda: The Story of Golda Meir*, illustrated by Donna Ruff, Puffin Books, New York, 1984. [Women of Our Time Biography]

Through the drama and scope of Golda Meir's life, including the years in the U.S., readers can gain an understanding of how the dream of a Jewish homeland came into reality. *Excellent biography.*

————, *The Children's Book of Jewish Holidays*, (Artscroll Youth Series), Mesorah Publications, New York, 1987.

Good one volume work on Jewish holidays for grades K–6.

Burstein, Chaya, A *Kids Catalog of Israel*, Jewish Publication Society of America, Philadelphia, 1988.

History, ethnic diversity, famous leaders, sights, sounds, holidays, recipes, activities; a wonderful way to explore Israel.

Chaikin, Miriam, *Ask Another Question: The Meaning of Passover*, Ticknor & Fields, 1986. *Sound the Shofar: The Story and Meaning of Rosh Hashannah and Yom Kippur*, Ticknor & Fields, 1986.

Presents origins, customs, traditions of Jewish holidays. Beautifully written. Other holidays available.

Drucker, Malka, *Hanukah: Eight Nights, Eight Lights*, Holiday House, New York, 1990.

Discusses origins, rituals of Hanukah, and Hanukah customs around the world. Beautifully written. Drucker has written books on Sabbath, Passover, etc., now out of print.

Finkelstein, Norman, *The Other 1492: Jewish Settlement in the New World*, Charles Scribner's Sons, New York, 1989.

> In 1492 Spanish Jews were expelled from their homes. Compelling telling of glorious world of Spanish Jews, their contributions to Spanish culture, their exile and beginnings of new lives in the New World.

Hurwitz, Johanna, *The Rabbi's Girls*, illustrated by Pamela Johnson, William Morrow & Comp., New York, 1982.

> Story takes place in Lorain, Ohio and is told by one of the rabbi's daughters; it shows how she feels about moving to a new town, about birth of a new sister, and at end of 1923, about the death of her father.

Kendall, Jonathan P., *My Name Is Rachamim*, illustrated by Alemu Eshetie, Union of American Hebrew Congregations, New York, 1987.

> The moving story of Ethiopian Jews; their life in Ethiopia, long trek to Sudan, eventual flight to Israel, and acclamation to their new homeland.

Morris, Ann (text) and Lilly Rubin (concept & photographs), *When Will the Fighting Stop? A Child's View of Jerusalem*, Antheneum, New York, 1990.

> A Jewish boy living in Jerusalem sees all the different people who make their homes there and wonders why they can't be friends. Beautifully conceived and executed.

Singer, Isaac Bashevis, *A Day of Pleasure: Stories of Boy Growing Up in Warsaw*, with photographs by Roman Vishniac, Farrar, Straus and Giroux, New York, 1986. National Book Award, 1970. [Nobel Laureate in Literature (Yiddish) in 1978]

> A memoir in stories of Singer's childhood in Poland, with all its richness, fun, variety; as told by a master storyteller.

———, *When Shlemiel Went to Warsaw & Other Stories*, illustrated by Margot Zemach, Farrar (et al), 1986. *Zlateh the Goat & Other Stories*, illustrated by Maurice Sendak, Harper, 1966. Newbery Honor Books

> Both wonderful collections of short stories set in Eastern Europe. Excellent to read aloud or alone.

Taylor, Sydney, *All-of-a-Kind Family. All-of-a-Kind Family Downtown. All-of-a-Kind Family Uptown. Ella of All-of-a-Kind Family. More All-of-a-Kind Family*, Taylor Productions, 1988 (hb; reprint); Dell, New York, 1980 (pb).

> First book, the adventures of five sisters growing up in Lower East Side, New York, turn of the century. Later books share more tales about them. *These have become classics.*

MIDDLE SCHOOL

Bamberger, David, *A Young Person's History of Israel*, Behrman House, New York, 1985.

> Excellent, readable presentation of the history of Israel based on Abba Eban's *My Country: The Story of Modern Israel.*

Cohen, Barbara, *King of the Seventh Grade*, Lothrup, Lee & Shepard, New York, 1983. National Jewish Book Award 1983.

> Novel of how it feels to be growing into a young teenager; especially good on feelings on becoming a Bar Mitzvah.

Gross, David C., *Justice for All Seasons, Louis D. Brandeis*, Lodestar Books (E. P. Dutton), 1987. (Jewish Biography Series)

> Biography of lawyer, judge, and worker for Zionist causes; first Jew on the Supreme Court; and man who helped end child labor in U.S.

Levinson, Nancy Smiler, *I Lift My Lamp, Emma Lazarus and the Statue of Liberty*, Lodestar Books (E. P. Dutton), New York, 1986.

> Biography of poet and writer from a prominent Sephardic (Spanish) Jewish family, who became a fighter for the causes of immigration and freedom, and whose poem is on the Statue of Liberty.

Lowry, Lois, *Number the Stars*, Houghton Mifflin Company, Boston, 1990. 1990 Newbery Medal.

> A sensitive novel of a ten year old Danish girl who helps shelter her Jewish friend from the Nazis. Book highlights Danish Resistance as they managed to smuggle almost all of the 7,000 Danish Jews to safety. Based largely on facts. *Superbly done.*

Meltzer, Milton, *The Jews in America: a Picture Album*, picture research by Rani Levinson, Jewish Publication Service of America, Philadelphia, 1985.

> American Jewish experience from the first settlers to the modern era, especially good on waves of immigration. Photos well chosen.

———, *Rescue: The Story of How Gentiles Saved Jews in the Holocaust*, Harper Collins, New York, 1988.

> Stories about "righteous gentiles" who risked their lives to rescue Jews during the Holocaust, by a leading author for teens.

Milgrim, Shirley, *Haym Salomon, Liberty's Son*, illustrated by Richard Fish, Jewish Publication Service of America, Philadelphia, 1975.

> Entertaining biography of little known Jewish merchant who helped finance the American Revolution.

Shamir, Ilana and Dr. Shlomo Shavit, editors, *The Young Reader's Encyclopedia of Jewish History*, Viking Kestrel, New York, 1987.

> One volume; history, culture, politics, war and peace, and religious issues come alive in well-written text with photos. Can be read as a narrative or used as a reference book.

Siegal, Aranka, *Upon the Head of a Goat, A Childhood in Hungary, 1939-1944*, Farrar, Straus, and Giroux, New York, 1981. Newbery Honor Book

> Based on author's childhood experiences; the story of a nine-year old and her family in Hungary during the Holocaust.

Siegel, Beatrice, *Lillian Wald of Henry Street*, Macmillan, Publishing Co., Inc., New York, 1983. (out of print, try to locate)

> Biography of an urban pioneer who developed new concepts in public health and pressed the government to take responsibility for the social welfare needs of people. Lillian Wald started the Henry Street Settlement.

Stadtler, Bea, *The Holocaust: A History of Courage and Resistance*, Behrman House, New York, 1974.

> Describes the experiences of Jews in Germany and the rest of Europe during twelve years of the Third Reich. Written

expressly for younger readers; includes focus on courage and resistance, with discussion questions. Recommended as a middle school text by the Ohio Council on Holocaust Education.

Strom, Yale, *A Tree Still Stands: Jewish Youth in Eastern Europe Today*, interviews and photographs by author, Philomel Books/The Putnam & Grosset Group, New York, 1990.

Interviews and photos of Jewish youth living in Eastern Europe. It explores thoughts on Judaism, assimilation, and non-Jewish attitudes.

Important book on life in newly emerging Eastern Block counties.

Syme, Daniel B., *The Jewish Home: A Guide for Jewish Living*, Jason Aronson Inc., Northvale, New Jersey, 1988.

Question/answer format makes this beautifully written book a good introduction to Jewish holiday and life cycle observances. An excellent resource for teachers and librarians; teens.

Volavkova, Hana, editor, *I Never Saw Another Butterfly: Children's Drawings and Poems from Terezin Concentration Camp, 1942-1944*, Schocken, 1987.

Teachers who ran the "model school" in Terezin encouraged their students to write and draw their feelings and hopes. A deeply moving book; suitable for middle school—adult.

HIGH SCHOOL

Bamberger, David, adaptor, *My People, Abba Eban's History of the Jews*, Vol. I & II, Behrman House, New York, 1978.

Well done adaptation for young teens of the outstanding history of the Jewish experience from ancient days to present. For older readers, consider the original.

Eban, Abba, *My Country: The Story of Modern Israel*, Random House, New York, 1972. (out of print, see Bamberger, David, Middle School.)

Moving narrative of the history of Israel by one of its most eloquent spokesmen. Though dated, one of the best on the earlier years.

Friedlander, Albert, editor, *Out of the Whirlwind: A Reader of Holocaust Literature*, illustrated by Jacob Landau, Schocken Books, New York, 1989.

> Anthology of selections from some of the best writings about the Holocaust by survivors and major thinkers on the topic. Would make an excellent high school/adult text.

Hapgood, Hutchins, *Spirit of the Ghetto: Studies of the Jewish Quarter of New York*, drawings from life by Jacob Epstein, Harvard University Press, Cambridge, 1967. (originally written 1904-1905)

> From 1898–1902 gifted writer Hapgood was given an assignment to go to Lower East Side, New York, and describe the customs and outlook of Jewish immigrants living in the ghetto. Book is a *classic*.

Howe, Irving, *World of Our Fathers*, with assistance from Kenneth Libo, Harcourt Brace Jovanovich, New York, 1989.

> Classic work on Eastern European Jewish immigrants, their move to Lower East Side, culture, economics, education, daily life, and adaptations to their new homes.

Klein, Gerda, *All But My Life*, Noonday, (Hill and Wang), New York, 1971.

> Holocaust survivor memoir, noted for hopeful outlook. *Highly recommended* for mature middle school to adult readers.

Meir, Golda, *My Life*, Dell, New York, 1976.

> Autobiography by an outstanding twentieth century leader, born in Eastern Europe, lived in the United States, and came alive in Palestine/State of Israel. Her life chronicles that of the state.

Meltzer, Milton, editor, *The Jewish Americans: A History in Their Own Words, 1650-1950*, Thomas Y. Crowell, New York, 1982

> In excerpts from diaries, letters, memoirs, speeches, etc., aided by excellent introductions by Meltzer, the reader is taken on a journey from the first Jewish settlement to 1950 in the United States.

————, *World of Our Fathers: The Jews of Eastern Europe*, Dell Publishing, 1974. *Taking Root: Jewish Immigrants in America*, Dell Publishing, New York, 1976. (out of print)

> Well-researched, highly-readable social histories, drawn from primary sources. Well worth the search. Meltzer makes history come alive and writes especially for teens.

Potok, Chaim, *The Chosen* (out of print), *The Promise*, Fawcett, New York, 1985. (look for *The Chosen*)

> Outstanding novel about relationships, fathers and sons, and friends. Set in the worlds of Hasidic Jews and Orthodox Jews in Brooklyn, New York; good introduction to traditional Judaism.

Roth, Henry, *Call It Sleep*, Farrar, Straus & Giroux, 1991, originally written in 1934.

> Considered the most distinguished work of fiction about immigrant life. About a young boy discovering himself. Set in Lower East Side in the early twentieth century.

Sharansky, Natan, *Fear No Evil*, translator Stefani Hoffman, Random House, New York, 1988.

> Autobiography of the famous former Soviet Jewish Refusenik; his years in prison in USSR, struggle to gain freedom and get to Israel, and eventual reunification with his wife. Symbol of Soviet Jewry struggles and triumph.

Steinberg, Milton, *Basic Judaism*, Harcourt, Brace, Jovanovich, New York, 1965, original copyright 1947.

> Still one of the best introductions to what the Jewish religion is all about. Highly recommended for high school/adult.

Wiesel, Elie, *Night*, Bantam Books, New York, 1982, original copyright, Farrar, Straus & Giroux, 1960. Author – Winner of Nobel Peace Prize – 1986.

> A penetrating, powerful account of teenage boy's experience in Nazi death camp. This most important work recalls evil at its absolute, and the message that horror like the Holocaust can never be allowed to happen again. *Must reading* for teen/adult.

Wyman, David S., *Abandonment of the Jews: America and the Holocaust, 1941-1945*, Pantheon, New York, 1986.

> Well-researched and documented, important book that analyzes the failure of the U. S. to respond to the desperate situation European Jews faced in World War II. Difficult, but *important*.

Yezierska, Anzia, *Bread Givers: A Novel*, *A struggle between a father of the Old World and a daughter of the New*, Persea Books, New York, 1975, original copyright 1925.

> Compelling exploration of tenement life, the struggle against poverty, family life and the need to break out of the ghetto. Superb exploration of a woman's view of the immigrant experience.

REFERENCES AND RESOURCES

Rabinsky, Leatrice B. and Carol Danks, co-editors, *The Holocaust: Prejudice Unleashed*, State of Ohio, 1989. Materials and Curriculum Committee of the Ohio Council on Holocaust Education.

> Well-done curriculum designed for use by high schools, includes readings, questions for discussion, and suggestions for further reading. A copy was sent to every high school in Ohio. For information, contact Dr. Herbert Hochhauser, Director of Ohio Council on Holocaust Education, Kent State University, Kent, OH 44242.

Levine, Rabbi Mark H., *Celebrating Jewish Heritage Week: Lesson Plans for Kindergarten through Sixth Grade*, designed by Joy Gold, Board of Jewish Education of Greater Washington, 11710 Hunters Lane, Rockville, MD 20852, 1991.

> May 3–May 10, 1992, is set aside by Congress to celebrate Jewish heritage. This well-designed publication for elementary (even to grade 7/8) schools provides specific miniunits to highlight the Jewish people's contributions to the United States. Five brief biographies with activities for the language arts curriculum for each grade. School can purchase one set and make copies.

ABOUT THE AUTHOR

Esther Cohen Hexter is director of the Educational Resource Center of the Akron Jewish Community Federation. She served as a member of the faculty of the Akron Jewish Community High School for twelve years. She was librarian of Beth El Synagogue Library for five years. In her capacity as Resource Center Director she is responsible for creating, expanding, and maintaining resources [book, media, display, game and curricula] in all areas of Judaica for use by area teachers, students, and community members; and for individual consultation with teachers and the design/running of teacher workshops. She is a writer, speaker, guest lecturer at area colleges and universities, workshop presenter, and adult education instructor.

9

"DEEP LIKE THE RIVERS"

BY ASHLEY BRYAN

My work has been in retelling and illustrating African folktales. I work from the sound of poetry to bring something of the spirit of the voice to the printed word and to try to open up that sense of hearing in reading that poetry allows. It is the sound of language that opens up the spirit of the oral tradition in the story. In Africa, story is theater: there's the involvement of the audience, there's the singing, the dancing, and the music, as I've tried to show in the illustrations for *The Dancing Granny*. When I'm writing, I want something of that spirit, that vitality, to come into the story.

In this chapter, I'll share with you how I go about working on a story by using examples from a number of black American poets, and then I hope you will see in the selection from one of my own

Reprinted with permission of Atheneum Publishers, an imprint of Macmillan Publishing Company from *The Dancing Granny* retold and illustrated by Ashley Bryan. Copyright © 1977 Ashley Bryan.

stories, the connection to poetry and theater.

To begin with, the title of this chapter is "Deep Like the Rivers," and it is taken from a Langston Hughes poem, "The Negro Speaks of Rivers."

> *I've known rivers:*
> *I've known rivers ancient as the world and older than the flow of human blood in human veins.*
> *My soul has grown deep like the rivers.*[1]

One of the exciting things that I open up to young people or to any audience, for that matter, is the idea that poetry is like song, that it's the form of literature that needs practice before being spoken. I often hold up a poem to my audience and show them it's just a few lines, but it can be a very big poem. It's the practice of the voice that really makes the poem come off the page. I like to begin with Langston Hughes, and a favorite of mine is "Dream Variations" because it has the spirit of dancing in it.[2]

Poets have a sensitive ear tuned to the speech of people, and Langston Hughes used the speech of his community and brought it into his poetry. He once did a series of twelve poems about a lady in Harlem. This lady has to stand up to all kinds of things that happen in her community. The wrong person comes knocking on her door and it's death, but she's not ready to entertain death. The census people ask her endless questions and she's bored with all these questions. The phone people say they're going to take out her phone because she hasn't paid the bill and she says, "You better leave my phone alone." In "Madam and the Rent Man" she's facing another person, and he is knocking, too, but she calls attention to her problems and refuses to give in to his demands.[3]

The exciting thing about working with poetry is that, although it contains the language we speak when we speak discursively, it brings us back to the vitality of sound, to the mystery and wonder of the words we use. The poet reminds us of the origins of language, so we're brought back again to the mystery that we can speak and understand, but the poet takes those words, recognizes their weight, and then, using the words in his or her own way, recreates language.

Paul Laurence Dunbar, who was born in 1872 in Dayton, Ohio, and died in 1906 at the age of 34, found his voice through the influence and inspiration of the English Romantic poets, Keats, Byron, and Shelley. He brought to that feeling of language his own rhythms and style. He used that sense of the loveliness of the Romantic spirit, and in his love poems this is so evident. Most of Dunbar's poems are in standard English, in the way he spoke, but it was for his dialect poems that he was most famous. Whenever he published a book of poetry his editors would pull out the dialect poems and publish them in separate illustrated books with photographs. These poems made him very popular. His books of dialect poems sold in the thousands, which is unusual in any age for poetry, but Dunbar always longed for more attention for his work in standard English. To fathom Dunbar's range as a poet it's important to read some of the poems in standard English as well as some he wrote in dialect. One of his love poems in standard English is titled "Roses and Pearls."[4]

To share one of the dialect poems with you, I've chosen a poem that's very popular with children. When Dunbar worked as a waiter at the Colombian World's Fair in 1892, he would hear the other waiters as they came through with their trays. They would kick the swinging doors open, and because there was such a crowd of waiters standing around talking about the lovely ladies they had met the day before, they would holler, "Jump back, honey. Jump back." The others would clear the space. Now Dunbar heard this over and over again, and so he took the refrain and used it in a dialect poem, "A Negro Love Song."

> *Seen my lady home las' night,*
> *Jump back, honey, jump back.*
> *Hel' huh han' an' sque'z it tight,*
> *Jump back, honey, jump back.*
> *Hyeahd huh sigh a little sigh,*
> *Seen a light gleam f'om huh eye,*
> *An' a smile go flittin' by-*

Jump back, honey, jump back.
Hyeahd de win' blow thoo de pine
Jump back, honey, jump back.
Mockin'-bird was singin' fine,
Jump back, honey, jump back.
An' my hea't was beatin' so,
When I reached my lady's do',
Dat I couldn't ba' to go-
Jump back, honey, jump back.

Put my ahm aroun' huh wais',
Jump back, honey, jump back.
Raised huh lips an' took a tase,
Jump back, honey, jump back.
Love me, honey, love me true?
Love me well ez I love you?
An' she answe'd, "'Cose I do"-
Jump back, honey, jump back.[5]

I also like to introduce Gwendolyn Brooks' *Bronzeville Boys and Girls* to children. Gwendolyn Brooks is the poet laureate of Illinois and the poetry consultant at the Library of Congress.

In *Bronzeville Boys and Girls* each poem is the name of a child who speaks out. These poems can be contrasted to some of the poems that capture the experiences of the teenagers in Gwendolyn Brooks' *Selective Poems*. Perhaps one of her most famous poems from this collection is "We Real Cool," which Brooks subtitled, "The Pool Players. Seven at the Golden Shovel."

We real cool. We
Left school. We

Lurk late. We
Strike straight. We

Sing sin. We
Thin gin. We

Jazz June. We
Die soon.[6]

Eight lines, but in those eight lines you can get across more about life in the inner city than hundreds of pages of a social studies text. Why is that? Because poetry deals with feelings, with the emotions; it forces you to admit that you do feel, that you do care. To remind students that they can feel and care is very helpful in enriching the material that teachers deal with in a textbook. The voice in "We Real Cool" is quite a contrast to the kind of innocence expressed in *Bronzeville Boys and Girls*.

Eloise Greenfield is another African American poet with such a strong voice that her poems sing on the page. "Things" is from *Honey, I Love.*

> *Went to the corner*
> *Walked in the store*
> *Bought me some candy*
> *Ain't got it no more*
> *Ain't got it no more*
>
> *Went to the beach*
> *Played on the shore*
> *Built me a sandhouse*
> *Ain't got it no more*
> *Ain't got it no more*
>
> *Went to the kitchen*
> *Lay down on the floor*
> *Made me a poem*
> *Still got it*
> *Still got it*[7]

When I do this poem with a group of children they say the words with me before I get through the poem once, and they beat out the rhythm. I often say that if you're working with children, you should give them at least a month to practice a poem before they speak it to a group. "Things" is one of those poems that doesn't take that long to work out; you can write it out and have choral reading right off. What I do is to say a line and have the children say it right after me. When I'm leaving a school where we've played with "Things" in this way, half the kids follow me out the door chanting "stee-eel got it."

This same spirit of sound and play is what I attempt to bring to the retelling of African folktales. In these stories I try to find a feeling of rhythm in the style to convey something of the oral tradition, so that what was once theater will be suggested through the vitality of play in the words. I began *The Cat's Purr* in this way.

> Once upon a time, Cat and Rat were the best of friends. Uh-huh, uh-huh, they really were! They lived in huts right next to each other. And since Rat liked to copy Cat, their huts matched.

> Cat planted a coconut palm tree by his hut. Rat planted one, too.

> Cat wove a straw mat for the corner of his hut. Rat wove one, too. When Rat visited Cat, he'd sit on Cat's mat; and on visits to Rat, Cat sat on Rat's mat.

> Cat made a bamboo flute and played sweet tunes.

> "Let me play a tune, too," said Rat.

> Cat let Rat play a tune, too: too-de-loo, too-de-loo.

> Cat and Rat farmed their land together. They worked in the field each day and took good care of their vegetable patch. After work they headed home, each with his hoe.

> One night, Cat's old uncle visited and brought Cat a present. Cat unwrapped the package. There, inside, was a small drum, the smallest drum Cat has ever seen.[8]

Scientists never have figured out what makes that sound when you stroke a cat. That "purrum, purrum." When I first came upon this story I knew right off that the drum that's embedded in this tale from the Antilles, that tells of why cat eats rat, is a marvelous invention for a storyteller to consider. I wanted to use the sound of the drum when I retold the story. Because I'm in the habit of trying out my ideas with the children I know on the little island where I live off the coast of Maine, I went to them and said, "Purrum, purrum. What does that sound like?" They told me right off, "You can't fool us; that's a cat purring." I knew then that I could use that bit in the *Cat's Purr* and so my telling of the tale was born. The story builds when rat comes and hears that sound and wants to play the drum. What follows is how we get the sound of the purring.

That spirit of the play of a voice is how I work with all stories, but this varies from story to story, of course. Among the Hausa people in Nigeria there is the story of a hen and frog. Many children are familiar with a story of the hen who goes out to plant some grain and asks the other animals to help her with the planting. Well, they refuse, of course, but when the bread is ready they're ready to eat, but now it's hen's turn to say "No, No, No." In this story from the Hausa, the audience anticipates what will happen, and this is one of the wonderful things that occurs while we read or listen to stories. Anticipation is one of the reasons why we read beautiful things over and over again, why we go again and again to the same plays, or to hear the same operas and symphonies. Through anticipation we recreate art. It becomes new even though you know it. You know the action, you know what's going to happen at the end, but as you anticipate you are doing something new with it each time. With the story of hen and frog the children can almost anticipate the action the first time through because they know the pattern, the pattern that is so deeply a part of their own experience. In my retelling of the tale which I titled "Hen and Frog,"[9] I try to make the pattern emerge out of the tale's music, its distinct voice—just as the poet would do it.

I'd like to close with just a reference to my work with the black American spirituals. These songs are in the hymnals of all the churches of our country. They are loved and sung throughout the world, but there were no books to introduce them to young people. I felt that was one reason why we don't have the variety in spirituals that should be available. When I lived in France and Germany, every year the songs of the people would come out once again. So I used block prints with the spirituals to give the collections the look

Reprinted with permission of Atheneum Publishers, an imprint of Macmillan Publishing Company from *I'm Going to Sing*, selected and illustrated by Ashley Bryan. Copyright © 1982 Ashley Bryan.

of early religious books. These songs are compared to a time in Western civilization when the great gothic cathedrals were created —the stained glass windows, the music, the sculptures, the illuminated manuscripts—all created for the greater glory of God. It is said that in Western culture that happened once again; it happened in this body of songs, the thousand or so spirituals that are now recorded. Because they're such beautiful songs they are part of the concert programs of many of our great singers. I felt there should be books devoted solely to these spirituals, not just the five or ten that you find in the popular folksong books, along with the English and Scotch or French and Irish ones. When I was working on this project, I worked it so that you could take a recorder or any melodic instrument and play a tune. I always include a few of the spirituals that I don't know, but which I've wanted to learn, in the books that I've done, *Walk Together Chil-*

dren and *I'm Going to Sing*. Because many children are being intro-
duced to music with the wooden flute or the recorder, I indicated
the notation so that the spirituals could be picked up on the flute
and then sung. I generally simplified the key so there aren't too
many sharps and flats to contend with. I'd like to close with one of
the spirituals, the very popular "Swing Low Sweet Chariot."[10]

Swing Low Sweet Chariot,
Comin for to Carry Me Home
Swing Low Sweet Chariot,...

NOTES:

1. Hughes, "The Negro Speaks of Rivers" from *Selected Poems of Langston Hughes*, 4. Copyright 1959 by Langston Hughes.

2. Hughes, "Dream Variations" from *Selected Poems of Langston Hughes*, 14.

3. Hughes, "Madam and the Rent Man" from *Selected Poems of Langston Hughes*, 204-05.

4. Dunbar, "Roses and Pearls" from *The Complete Poems of Paul Laurence Dunbar*, 447.

5. Dunbar, "A Negro Love Song" from *The Paul Laurence Dunbar Reader*, 292. Copyright 1975 by Jay Martin and Gossie H. Hudson. Reprinted by permission of Dodd, Mead & Company.

6. Brooks, "We Real Cool" from *Selected Poems*, 73. Copyright 1963 by Gwendolyn Brooks. Reprinted by permission of Harper & Row, Publishers.

7. Greenfield, "Things" from *Honey, I Love*. Copyright 1978 by Eloise Greenfield. Reprinted by permission of Harper & Row, Publishers.

8. Bryan, *The Cat's Purr*, 3-5; 7. Copyright 1985 by Ashley Bryan. Reprinted by permission of Atheneum, an imprint of the Macmillan Publishing Company.

9. Bryan, "Hen and Frog" from *Beat the Story Drum, Pum-Pum*.

10. Bryan, "Swing Low Sweet Chariot" from *Walk Together Children*, 43.

WORKS CITED:

Brooks, Gwendolyn. *Bronzeville Boys and Girls*. Illustrated by Ronni Solbert. New York: Harper & Row, 1956.

———. *Selected Poems*. New York: Harper & Row, 1963.

Bryan, Ashley. *Beat the Story Drum, Pum-Pum*. New York: Atheneum, 1980.

———. *The Cat's Purr*. New York: Atheneum, 1985.

———. *Walk Together Children*. New York: Atheneum, 1974.

Dunbar, Paul Laurence. *The Complete Poems of Paul Laurence Dunbar*. New York: Dodd, Mead & Company, 1970.

Greenfield, Eloise. *Honey, I Love and Other Love Poems*. Illustrated by Diane and Leo Dillon. New York: Thomas Y. Crowell, 1978.

Hughes, Langston. *Selected Poems of Langston Hughes*. New York: Vintage Classics, 1990.

Martin, Jay, and Gossie H. Hudson, eds. *The Paul Laurence Dunbar Reader*. New York: Dodd, Mead & Company, 1975.

ADDITIONAL BOOKS WRITTEN AND ILLUSTRATED BY ASHLEY BRYAN:

All Night, All Day: A Child's First Book of African-American Spirituals. New York: Atheneum, 1991.

The Dancing Granny. New York: Macmillan, 1987.

Lion and the Ostrich Chick & Other African Folk Tales. New York: Macmillan, 1986.

Sh-Ko & His Eight Wicked Brothers. New York: Macmillan, 1988.

Turtle Knows Your Name. New York: Macmillan, 1989.

ABOUT THE AUTHOR

Inspired by the rich oral tradition of African storytelling and the rhythms of African American poetry, Ashley Bryan has retold and illustrated numerous African folktales and black American spirituals, many of which have received starred reviews and other honors. A graduate of the Cooper Union Art School, he taught painting and drawing at Dartmouth College for many years, and he frequently lectures and performs at conferences and schools across the country. About his books he has said, "I hope my work with the African tales will be, by the very nature of storytelling, like a "tender bridge" reaching across distances of time and space." Mr. Bryan is the recipient of the 1991 Hope S. Dean Award from The Foundation for Children's Books. He lives on a small island off the coast of Maine.

10

WORD MAGIC

BY BARBARA JUSTER ESBENSEN

Whether I am reading stories and poems written by others or struggling to get one of my own efforts in readable shape, it is the quality of the language that interests me most. I look for this "language" in every book I read. I look for the magical transformation of mere words into living images for the mind to catch and hold onto.

Over the past few years, I have been the "reteller" of two Ojibway tales, a Seneca legend, and a collection of ancient Latvian folksongs called *dainas*. I am not Native American nor am I Latvian. Yet, when I am asked whether or not this fact makes a difference in the way the original material is interpreted, I say, "No. I don't think so."

I read the "Legend of the Water Lily" in the leatherette-bound copy of *My Bookhouse*, volume 2, when I was only eight or nine years old, back in the 1930s. Many years later, as the mother of many children—five at the time—I had been looking for this story to read to my young family, but could never find it again.

Then, one summer, we traveled back to my Madison, Wisconsin, home with the kids, and I remembered to ask my mother if the *Bookhouse* books were still around. To my surprise, they were all packed away in a box in her attic, and I immediately claimed them for myself.

In re-reading it, I found that I was still enchanted with this legend of the star who yearns to live on earth so she can be near the Ojibway people. But I saw, too, that it was a very spare version indeed. It relied on "telling about" instead of "showing" the events through images and descriptive language.

The tale in my old book tells us that a young brave has a dream. It says that "A lovely maiden, white and silvery as the star seemed to stand at his side and she said..."[1]

I found that as I read this old story again, I could hear her voice saying the familiar words—just as I could hear it long ago as a child. What I heard was not an everyday human voice, but the ethereal voice of a star-come-to-earth. Perhaps over the centuries when this story was told to a group of listeners, the Ojibway storyteller spoke the star's words with a special intonation.

My job as a writer is to give a sense of this other worldly voice, using the only tools I have—words. In *The Star Maiden*, it says:

That very night
one of those young braves
had a dream. A silver maiden
came into his dream.
She shone with silver light.
She spoke to him. Her voice was like
a thread of silver.
She held out her shining arms to him...[2]

Later in the story, the Star Maiden calls out to her sisters in the sky to join her on earth. She speaks to their reflections in the water of the lake. The original text then tells us "...the next morning the Indians found hundreds of beautiful white water lilies floating bright on the surface of the lake."[3]

This seemed too abrupt to me. I wanted some response from the stars who have listened to her plea. My story tells us:

*"The people saw the sky shake
with glittering points of light.
They saw the lake come alive
with stars..."*[4]

I see my job as a reteller of these traditional stories to be one of *showing* instead of merely *telling* the reader *about* the action of the tale. I want the reader's response to be a visual one. I hope the reader feels as though the story has, indeed "come alive..."

When Little, Brown accepted *The Star Maiden*, they asked me to research the true origins of this legend, if possible. But the citation in *My Bookhouse* was simply "An Ojibway tale."

Once more, I am indebted to the astounding knowledge of librarians! When I went to the Minneapolis Public Library and told them my charge from Little, Brown, Lois Ringquist, assistant head of Children's Services immediately went to work.

Before long, she unearthed an old book, published in 1850. It had been written by an Ojibway chief, Keh-ge-ga-gah-bowh, who later took the name, George Copway. His book, called *The Traditional History and Characteristic Sketches of the Ojibway Nation*, set down Ojibway history, customs, and legends. His fear was that if he did not do this, the information would one day disappear entirely.

I found my water lily story there. It had been taken from this old work almost word-for-word and published in *My Bookhouse*. As I browsed through the 1850s book, I came across many fascinating things. And most important to me was the discovery of the legend that tells why native peoples learned to treat disease and common illnesses with plants and herbs. This is the story I have called *Ladder to the Sky*.

In this story, there is a forbidden vine that connects earth to the great Spirit's heavenly realm. In the original, the writer states:

> The chief men had enjoined on all the duty to refrain from any desire or any attempt to ascend the vine whose branches reached the heavens, telling them that to do so would bring upon them severe penalties.[5]

In *Ladder to the Sky* the story tells us about:

...the magic vine that grew in the very center
of the Ojibway lands.
The vine grew in the earth,
but its far-off top was looped around a star.
...The Ojibway people were forbidden to touch
this magic vine.
It was a living ladder connecting the earth
with Manitou's great blue sky home.[6]

Later in the story, an old woman does climb the vine to bring back her grandson. In the chief's telling, the woman, "after nightfall repaired to the vine and began to ascend it..."[7]

Wanting to make this scene more dramatic in my book, I describe it like this:

When darkness fell on the village,
the grandmother crept along the forest edge
until she reached the forbidden vine.
When she came near the vine,
it began to give off a wild light,
and a force from within it
seemed to be pushing her away.

But old women have a force of their own.
She broke through the power of the vine
and wrapped her arms around its cold stem."[8]

Recently, I retold another Native American tale—Seneca this time. Again, the original source was a Native American, Arthur C. Parker (Gawaso Wanneh), whose father and grandfather were Seneca chieftains. He took down the stories for his book, *Skunny Wundy*, as his father and other tribal elders related them during long winter evenings of storytelling.

Once again, I was struck by the difference between a story that is told orally, with gestures, facial expressions, and changing tone-of-voice, and a story that must end up being understandable and compelling through words alone.

Literature is not, as I've said before, merely the relating of events. Literature must place the reader inside the story, using nothing but words— words that can be found in any dictionary, on any word-list, or inside one's own head. The "magic" happens when the words are allowed to combine, one with another, until the scene is set, the picture is painted, the voices of the characters are clearly heard in all their individuality.

The little four-line Latvian *dainas* I mentioned earlier were sent to me by a Latvian writer I met during a reception for former Soviet writers and illustrators of children's books. They were visiting the Kerlan Library on the campus of the University of Minnesota. The Latvian gentleman, learning that I had retold *The Star Maiden*, asked if I would be interested in retelling some of these ancient folksongs in whatever form I would choose for them. I said I would be thrilled to have the chance to try my hand at this challenge.

When the collection of 150 *dainas* arrived, I was astounded to see that they covered just about every possible idea and event that could occur in one's lifetime. The lines talked about love, marriage, death, farm life, city life, holidays and celebrations, spells and remedies, women's work, men's work, joy, sorrow, disappointments, trickery, soldiering—an almost endless list.

I wondered how I could possibly connect all these various things in a coherent way. Then, reading one *daina* after another, I came upon these lines:

> *The mouse drives.*
> *The cart creaks with its load*
> *of sleep.*[9]

As you can imagine, this collection of "mere words" sparkled all by itself on the page in front of me! I then found wonderful lines about fishing, weaving, otters, marsh marigolds, colorful petticoats, and the myths about the weather, the sun, the moon, their children, and even their marriages. What a book full of riches had been sent to me!

Last winter, I showed the finished book, *The Dream Mouse*, to an elderly Latvian woman who had seen an article I had written on this attempt to make a children's book out of the *dainas*. She said that I had "entered the *dainas* and found the exact voice for the telling..." She said I "sounded Latvian," which certainly pleased me. As a university student in Riga, during the 1920s, she had been one of the many young people who, for more than fifty years—since the 1870s—had been sent out to collect these disappearing bits of folk wisdom and song.

And a former teacher at a Native American school in the Minneapolis area told me that my retellings "have the Ojibway tone to them. Your stories have the same 'voice' we heard at our school when an Ojibway elder came to school and gave us the legends in the old storytelling way..." Again, you can imagine how delighted I was to hear this.

It seems to me that if one tries to have a real sensitivity to the "voice" of a culture not one's own, and if one combines this with the ability to use language in the most powerful ways possible, the resulting retelling will be valid and satisfying.

At least this is what I have tried to do, and what I will continue to attempt as I find other marvelous tales to offer to the children of today. Like all writers, I am a trafficker in the most powerful and delightful magic of all—word magic!

NOTES:

1. Miller, *My Bookhouse*.

2. Esbensen, *The Star Maiden*. Text copyright © 1988 by Barbara Juster Esbensen. Reprinted by permission of Little, Brown and Co.

3. Millie, *My Bookhouse*.

4. Esbensen, *The Star Maiden*. Reprinted by permission of Little, Brown and Co.

5. Copway. *The Traditional History and Characteristic Sketches of the Ojibway Nation*.

6. Esbensen, *Ladder to the Sky*. Text copyright © 1989 by Barbara Juster Esbensen. Reprinted by permission of Little, Brown and Co.

7. Copway, *The Traditional History and Characteristic Sketches of the Ojibway Nation*.

8. Esbensen, *Ladder to the Sky*. Reprinted by permission of Little, Brown and Co.

9. Esbensen, *The Dream Mouse*.

WORKS CITED:

Copway, George (Chief of the Ojibway Nation, Keh-ge-ga-gah-bowh). *The Traditional History and Characteristic Sketches of the Ojibway Nation*. London: Charles Gilpin, 1850.

Parker, Arthur C. *Skunny Wundy Seneca Indian Tales*. Ill. by George Armstrong. New York: George H. Doran, 1926.

Miller, Olive Beaupre. *My Bookhouse*, volume 2. Chicago: Bookhouse for Children, 1925.

A SELECTED LISTING OF BOOKS BY BARBARA JUSTER ESBENSEN:

Cold Stars and Fireflies: Poems of the Four Seasons. Ill. by Susan Bonners. New York: Crowell, 1984.

The Dream Mouse. (forthcoming)

Great Northern Diver: The Loon. Ill. by Mary Barrett Brown. Boston: Little, Brown, 1990.

Ladder to the Sky: How the Gift of Healing Came to the Ojibway Nation (retold). Ill. by Judith K. Davie. Boston: Little, Brown, 1989.

Who Shrank My Grandmother's House Poems of Discovery. Ill. by Eric Beddows. New York: HarperCollins, 1992.

The Star Maiden (retold). Ill. by Judith K. Davie. Boston: Little, Brown, 1988.

Tiger with Wings: The Great Horned Owl. Ill. by Mary Barrett Brown. New York: Orchard, 1991.

Words with Wrinkled Knees. Ill. by John Stadler. New York: Crowell, 1986.

ABOUT THE AUTHOR

Barbara Esbensen is a writer and teacher who has lived and worked in many parts of the United States. She has taught both art and creative writing, but has always been a writer first. Her first book, *Swing Around the Sun*, is a book of poetry and was published in 1965. She has published many other works of poetry and is currently working on several projects, with publication planned for next year. She lives with her husband Thorwald, who is also a writer and former educator.

11

THE AFRICAN AMERICAN FOLKTALE IN THE PRIMARY CLASSROOM

BY DARWIN L. HENDERSON

Summer nights on the front porch
Aunt Sue cuddles a brown-faced child to her bosom
And tells him stories.[1]

The Langston Hughes poem "Aunt Sue's Stories," offers a gentle and nurturing introduction to the beauty of the African American oral tradition. It is a tradition where story is all important with elements which authentically and accurately reflect an African American heritage. Furthermore, it is a tradition in which story has the power to inform, guide, and strengthen and provides a foundation for an African American literary heritage.

The African American folktale, prose in narrative form, multi-patterned and multi-faceted, lies at the root of the culture. At the heart of these stories is the cultural truth—the truth of experience as the ancient storyteller knew it. These stories are reflected cultural history embedded in as Rudine Sims Bishop states, "...an Afro-American sensibility...rooted in a traditional African world view."[2] It is this African world view which emphasizes harmony and a belief in the highly ordered and cyclical rhythm of the universe.[3]

Children in the primary grades are especially interested in folktales because the tales provide pleasure and enjoyment. Likewise, the tales are popular because their structure allows children to identify and empathize with the characters.

Developmentally, children's interest in folktales is at a peak between the approximate ages of six and eight.[4] Andre Favat describes the child's interest in folktales as corresponding to the stages of development set forth by Swiss psychologist, Jean Piaget. Among Favat's conclusions: young children often believe objects and animals have life or magical qualities similar to those found in folktales. Further, folktales enable children's sense of what is just and they can clearly distinguish between good and evil characters. According to Favat, children's interest in folktales emerges during kindergarten and declines around fifth grade, when children are less egocentric.[5]

Therefore, the use of the African American folktale in the primary classroom is important during this peak of interest. Tales from the oral tradition help to enhance children's growing understanding of the world. Among the many values of using the tales with children outlined in Ruth Kearney Carlson are several which directly apply to African American folktales. Carlson states that tales foster children's appreciation for cultures different from their own. She also states that tales encourage children to realize the various positive human qualities which all people possess.[6]

In addition to these values, the tales foster the pride of, and heighten the self-concept of the African American child. Children from parallel cultures can develop respect for the history, culture, and various contributions made by African Americans through the use of folktales.

When beginning a unit of study on African American folktales, it is vital to start with tales which have been a part of the African oral tradition. Through centuries of telling, these stories reveal the beliefs, values and relevant cultural patterns of an ancient world.

While there are numerous illustrated picture books which contain a single folktale, teachers may want to begin with several which clearly draw upon traditional values and beliefs of various African cultures. The most notable of these is Jan Carew's *The Third Gift*. Carew tells of how Jubas, a clan of herdsmen and warriors, acquired the three most important gifts of humanity—work, beauty and imagination. The tale is set in "long time past days" and is told in a graceful flowing style reminiscent of oral storytelling. Its length should not discourage read aloud, and would be a good choice to read in two installments, if time did not permit a single reading.

Another folktale rich in oral tradition is Gail Haley's *A Story, A Story*. This is the perfect introduction to the African trickster, Ananse the spider man, who uses wit to overcome various obstacles to acquire the sky god's stories. Birago Diop's *Mother Crocodile*, as translated and adapted by Rosa Guy, shows the necessity of children listening to their parents and elders in the face of danger.

These specific tales deal with the qualities that reappear throughout most African cultures' beliefs and values. These are qualities that have formed a cultural and literary bridge to America, where the same feelings about human and spiritual conditions reappear in the African American experience and are reflected in folktales.

Through the experience of slavery in North America, Africans formed new folktales. In her introduction to *The People Could Fly: American Black Folk Tales*, Virginia Hamilton states that the slave experience and the "combined...memories and habits from the old world of Africa" produced a new "body of folk expression..."[7] Widely known and beautifully crafted, this collection of 24 tales reflects the range of stories representing the body of African American folk literature.

Several collections will add depth as well as pleasure to the unit of study. One is Hamilton's book, and other is William J. Faulkner's *The Days When the Animals Talked*. The 34 tales are similar in tone to Joel Chandler Harris' "Uncle Remus" stories, although more readable. These are stories Faulkner heard as boy growing up on a Virginia farm, told by the former slave, Simon Brown.

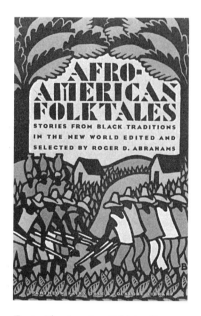

From *Afro-American Folktales*. Copyright © 1985 by Roger D. Abrahams. Reprinted with permission of Pantheon Books, a division of Random House, Inc.

Finally, some teachers might find Roger D. Abrahams' *Afro-American Folktales*, an excellent resource for additional non-illustrated tales. Abrahams' preface and introduction will give folktale enthusiasts detailed and insightful information regarding the tales' embedded cultural importance.

Priscilla Jaquith's *Bo Rabbit Smart for True: Folktales from the Gullah* contains four stories from the sea islands off the coast of Georgia and South Carolina. The Gullah language is a blend of Elizabethan English, African languages, and dialect expressions from various British provinces. This combination of language and experience has produced stories which are lilting and lively in humor.

Patricia McKissack's *Flossie & the Fox* could easily be considered a modern folktale. The author has used the full flavor of her grandfather's storytelling, to weave the story of Flossie Finley who outsmarts the master trickster—the fox. The language is rich, vibrant, and full of the color of Southern African American speech.

The great American hero, John Henry, is the subject of several books appropriate for use in the primary classroom. Ezra Jack Keats' *John Henry: An American Hero* portrays John Henry as the energetic, powerful, larger-than-life steel drivin' man as we have come to know him. Steve Sanfield's *A Natural Man: The True Story of John Henry* is a longer, lyrical treatment. Sanfield's John Henry tells the reader "I'm a natural man, and I can't help it,"[8] in reference to his physical skill and talents. Sanfield includes many railroad workgang chants in this version. At the conclusion of the tale, he provides music and lyrics to "The Ballad of John Henry."

These two aspects of Sanfield's telling are invitations for reader interaction with the tale.

Three recent retellings by Robert D. San Souci capture delight and drama that only folktales can cast. In *The Talking Eggs*, San Souci weaves a tale adapted from a Louisiana Creole legend rooted in European fairy tales. Here, kindness, magic and miracle have the power to transform. In the author's note of *The Boy and the Ghost*, San Souci informs the reader that the idea for this story of "a boy visiting a haunted house and meeting up with a ghost"[9] came from two short African American ghost stories recorded around the turn of the century. In this version, the "good, brave lad"[10] sets the ghost free and brings a hidden treasure back to his family. Finally, *Sukey and the Mermaid* is a story from a fragment of an authentic folktale involving mermaids. Set in "a little island off the coast of South Carolina,"[11] Sukey encounters a mermaid, Mama Jo, who answers her song and grants her wishes which change her life through kindness and magic.

San Souci, a master storyteller, has become a major voice in the retelling of obscure fragments of these distinctive African American tales. As he finds fragments, he continues to explore various other related folkways and stories. Masterfully, he recreates tales which adhere to the fragments of the historical past and then embellishes them with cultural authenticity.

The African American folktale has a very broad appeal and range. Primary school children will ask for these stories repeatedly. As previously stated, they are rooted in a traditionally African world view, and form an African American sensibility. As Jane Yolen states, they hold "culture in the mouth."[12] This Ethiopian proverb voices nearly the same thought:

"When the heart overflows, it comes out through the mouth."[13]

NOTES:

1. Hughes, *The Selected Poems*.

2. Sims, *Substance and Shadow*, 50.

3. Ibid., 50

4. Favat, *Child and Tale: The Origins of Interest*.

5. Ibid.

6. Carlson, "World Understanding Through Folktale." In *Folklore and Folktales Around the World*.

7. Hamilton, *The People Could Fly: American Black Folktales*, x.

8. Sanfield, *A Natural Man: The True Story of John Henry*, 26.

9. San Souci, *The Boy and the Ghost*, (unnumbered)

10. Ibid., (unnumbered)

11. San Souci, *Sukey and the Mermaid*, (unnumbered)

12. Yolen, *Favorite Folktales from Around the World*, 11.

13. Leslau, *African Proverbs*, 23.

WORKS CITED:

Abrahams, Roger D., Editor. *Afro-American Folktales: Stories from Black Traditions in the New World*. New York: Pantheon, 1984.

Carew, Jan. *The Third Gift*. Illustrated by Leo and Diane Dillon. Boston: Little, Brown, 1974.

Diop, Birago. *Mother Crocodile*. Translated and adapted by Rosa Guy. Illustrated by John Steptoe. New York: Delacorte, 1981.

Faulkner, William J. *The Days When the Animals Talked: Black American Folktales and How They Came to Be*. Illustrated by Troy Howell. Chicago: Follett, 1977.

Hamilton, Virginia. *The People Could Fly: American Black Folktales*. Illustrated by Leo and Diane Dillon. New York: Knopf, 1985.

Jaquith, Priscilla. *Bo Rabbit Smart for True: Folktales from the Gullah*. Drawings by Ed Young. New York: Philomel, 1981.

Keats, Ezra Jack. *John Henry: An American Legend*. New York: Knopf, 1965.

Leslau, Charlotte and Wolf, compilers. *African Proverbs*. Decorations by Jeff Hill. White Plains, New York: Peter Pauper Press, 1985.

McKissack, Patricia C. *Flossie & the Fox*. Illustrated by Rachel Isadora. New York: Dial, 1986.

Sanfield, Steve. *A Natural Man: The True Story of John Henry*. Illustrated by Peter J. Thornton. Boston: David R. Godine, 1986.

Sims, Rudine. *Shadow and Substance: Afro-American Experience in Contemporary Children's Fiction*. Urbana, Illinois: National Council of the Teachers of English, 1982.

San Souci, Robert D. *The Boy and the Ghost*. Illustrated by Brian Pinkney. New York: Simon and Schuster, 1989.

———. *Sukey and the Mermaid*. Illustrated by Brian Pinkney. New York: Four Winds, 1992.

———. *The Talking Eggs*. Illustrated by Jerry Pinkney. New York: Dial, 1989.

Yolen, Jane, editor. *Favorite Folktales from around the World*. New York: Pantheon, 1986.

ABOUT THE AUTHOR

Darwin Henderson teaches children's literature in the School of Education at Purdue University. His area of interest is African American literature for children and young adults.

APPENDIX A

A SELECTED LISTING OF MULTICULTURAL TRADE BOOKS FOR CHILDREN AND YOUNG ADULTS

EDITED BY IONE COWEN

In the following bibliography, we have tried to represent the increasingly broad understanding of multiculturalism which the Conference now endorses. Members of the Virginia Hamilton Advisory Board were invited to submit favorite titles used in their own teaching, storytelling, or other work with children and young adults.

All entries are coded for age/grade level with a letter code following the ISBN number. **K - Kindergarten**, **P - Preschool**, **I - Intermediate**, **J - Junior High**, **S - Senior High**. When books are also useful as a professional resource, this is indicated by the word "Professional."

> Adoff, Arnold. *Black Is Brown Is Tan*. Illustrated by Emily McCully. Harper and Row, 1973. (0-06-020083-9) P
>
> > Two mischievous young children share a house filled with the love of their brown-skinned mama and their white-skinned daddy. This portrait of a mixed-race family is full of life and perfect for reading aloud.

Armstrong, Jennifer. *Steal Away.* Orchard, 1992. (0-531-05983-9) J

This exciting and emotionally-charged account of two young women, one a slave and the other a slave owner, tells of their attempt to flee the unbearable conditions of bondage.

Ashabranner, Brent and Ashabranner, Melissa. *Into a Strange Land.* Dodd, Mead, 1987. (0-399-21709-6) I -J

The stories of unaccompanied refugee youth from Southeast Asia are told in a combination of words and photographs. The authors include interviews with foster parents, social workers and government officials, but the most moving words come from the refugees themselves. The work blends information and sensitive reporting as it documents the courage of this group of young immigrants.

Bode, Janet. *New Kids on the Block: Oral Histories of Immigrant Teens.* Franklin Watts, 1989. (0-531-10794-9) J - S

Oral accounts of teenage immigrants help the reader come to understand the emotional impact associated with fleeing from one's homeland and adjusting to a new life in the United States.

Bruchac, Joseph and London, Jonathan, editors. *Thirteen Moons on Turtle's Back: A Native American Year of Moons.* Illustrated by Thomas Locker. Philomel Books, 1992. (0-399-22141-7) P - I - J

A collection of poetry related to the thirteen moons of the year as they are known by Native Americans. Locker's exquisite illustrations add depth and dimension.

Buss, Fran Leeper. *Journey of the Sparrows.* Lodestar, 1991. (0-525-67362-8) J - S

Maria's journey from El Salvador to Chicago with her brother and sister is a mixed blessing. Although they will leave behind the violence that has transformed their native country, they must now survive as illegal immigrants, separated from the rest of their family.

Caduto, Michael J. and Joseph Bruchac. *Keepers of the Earth: Native American Stories and Environmental Activities for Children.* Illustrated by John K. Fadden and Carol Wood. Fulcrum Publishing, 1988. (1-55591-027-0) I - J - S - Professional

> This unusual combination of stories and related activities is intended to stimulate curiosity and the process of discovery. Reading the Dakota story, "How Turtle Flew South for the Winter," leads to a discussion of migration, hibernation and the pattern of the seasons. The approach involves senses, thoughts and action as expressed through dramatics, writing, creative arts, and science.

Caines, Jeanette. *Just Us Women*. Illustrated by Pat Cummings. Harper and Row, 1982. (0-06-020941-0) K - P

> The illustrations intensify the point of view as well as the special relationship between the two "women." Racially and gender wise, it is most effective.

Chang, Ina. *A Separate Battle: Women and the Civil War*. Lodestar, 1991. (0-525-67365-2) I - J - S

> In addition to providing a well-documented and spirited survey of women's various roles during the Civil War, Chang focuses on the specific and enduring contributions of Harriet Tubman, Clara Barton, and other notables whose convictions took shape in courageous, often humbling, work. This is history made vivid, accessible, and gripping.

Choi, Sook Nyul. *Year of Impossible Goodbyes*. Houghton Mifflin, 1991. (0-395-57419-6) I - J

> While living in northern Korea during the turbulent period of the Second World War, ten-year-old Sookan and others in her extended family must endure the vicious tactics of the Japanese military and, once the war ends in 1945, the unceasing and cunning terrorism imposed by Communist Russian troops. Aided by a resister, Sookan and her younger brother make a treacherous escape to South Korea and the promise of freedom.

Clifton, Lucille. *Three Wishes*. Illustrated by Michael Hays. Doubleday, 1992. (0-385-30497-8) K - P

> Finding a penny on New Year's Day with her birthday year on it, gives a young girl three wishes. As each of her wishes comes true, Nobie discovers how important friendship really is.

Crew, Linda. *Children of the River*. Delacorte, 1989. (0-440-50122-9) S

Seventeen year old Sundara is torn between remaining faithful to her Cambodian heritage and adjusting to life in an Oregon high school as an American. This dramatic tale combines and contrasts hope, loss, courage and love as it portrays the young girl's struggles to balance the demands and expectations of these diverse cultures.

Crews, Donald. *Bigmama's*. Greenwillow, 1991. (0-688-09950-5) K - P

Visiting Bigmama's house in Florida is the best way to spend the hot, endless days of summer because there are so many things to do, places to explore, and friends and family to enjoy.

Cummings, Pat. *Clean Your Room, Harvey Moon*. Bradbury, 1991. (0-02-725511-5) K - P

Because Harvey's room is such a mess, his mother insists he clean it on Saturday morning—of all times! His method of dealing with socks, marbles, trains, and things icky and sticky is ingenious, but less than satisfactory to Mom.

Dragonwagon, Crescent. *Home Place*. Illustrated by Jerry Pinkney. Macmillan, 1990. (0-02-733190-3) K - P - I

Images of a home long ago are imagined by a family hiking through the woods on a sunny day. Pinkney's watercolor illustrations capture the spirit of an African American family's home which is only a memory, except for a chimney and rows of yellow daffodils.

Durham, Michael. *Powerful Days: The Civil Rights*. Photography of Charles Moore. Stewart, Tabori and Chang, 1991. (1-55670-171-3) J - S

Charles Moore chronicled the civil rights struggle for *Life Magazine* and his arresting photographs cover the movement beginning with James Meredith's court-ordered admission to the University of Mississippi in 1962.

Poignant commentary is written by Michael Durham, the reporter with whom Moore worked on several assignments.

Friedman, Ina R. *How My Parents Learned to Eat*. Illustrated by Allen Say. Houghton, Mifflin, 1984. (0-395-35379-3) K - P

> The cultural differences between an American sailor and Japanese girl are shown by the fact they are unable to use one another's table utensils. A young girl tells how her parents overcame this obstacle as she explains why some days their family eats with chopsticks and some days with knives and forks. The colorful illustrations reinforce the gentle humor of the text as love blossoms in this meeting of East and West.

Giovanni, Nikki. *Spin a Soft Black Song*, rev. ed. Illustrated by George Martins. Hill and Wang, 1985. (0-8090-8796-0) P - I - J

> Ingenuous wit and wisdom highlight these free verse poems about African American children on such homey subjects as "Let's Take a Nap," "Shopping" and "Trips." Soft pencil drawings compliment the simple themes of this moving poetry collection accessible to children of all ages.

Greenfield, Eloise. *First Pink Light*. Illustrated by Jan Spivey Gilchrist. Black Butterfly, 1991. (0-86316-207-X) K - P

> Tyree's mother lovingly allows him to sit in a special chair where he will be able to see the first pink light of dawn as he waits for his father to return home.

———. *Night on Neighborhood Street*. Illustrated by Jan Spivey Gilchrist. Dial, 1991. (0-8037-0777-0) K - P I

> Whether it is Nerissa cheering her out of work father and sick mother or Tonya's mother blowing lullaby sounds into the silent night air, this gentle and beautiful poetry collection gives readers a real sense of family strength and community ties.

Hamilton, Virginia. *The People Could Fly: American Black Folktales*. Illustrated by Leo and Diane Dillon. Knopf, 1985. (0-394-86925-7) P - I - J - S

> More than 20 historical slave tales are compellingly told and beautifully illustrated. The author writes the tales to be read aloud, as if she herself were speaking them. They are divided into sections reflecting the belief that African American slaves used the stories to express emotions and support while entertaining each other.

Haseley, Dennis. *Ghost Catcher*. Illustrated by Lloyd Bloom. HarperCollins Children's Books, 1991. (0-06-022244-1) J - S

> When Ghost Catcher, the village's solitary, mysterious, and emotionally bereft altruist, becomes trapped in the dark side of life, he is rescued from his despair through the unconditional love of his village friends. Bloom's arresting illustrations, rendered in the manner of Diego Rivera's warm textures and vibrant colors, bring to light the implications of a symbolic tale steeped in the wisdom and rhythms of Latin American oral traditions.

Haskins, Jim. *One More River to Cross: Twelve Black Americans*. Scholastic, 1992. (0-590-42896-9) J - S

> The African Americans whose stories Haskins tells were forced to surmount many obstacles on their way to realizing their personal dreams or their struggle to secure equal rights for other Black people. Celebrated are the achievements of such gifted and determined individuals as Crispus Attucks, a Revolutionary War hero; Madam C. J. Walker, the first American woman to earn a million dollars; Fannie Lou Hammer, the civil rights activist; and Ronald McNair, an astronaut who died in the Challenger tragedy.

Ho, Minfong. *The Clay Marble*. Farrar, Straus and Giroux, 1991. (0-374-31340-7) I - J

> To escape the horrors of the Cambodian war, Dara and her family flee to a refugee camp. The reader feels the family's fear as it makes its escape, forever transformed by having seen the brutality of war, and witnesses the precarious existence the family must now eke out for as long as it takes for the wounds of war to heal.

Hoffman, Mary. *Amazing Grace*. Illustrated by Caroline Binch. Dial, 1991. (0-8037-1040-2) K - P

> The only word for Grace is amazing. Here is a child who loves stories and whose active imagination knows no bounds. Supported by her family, she becomes Joan of Arc, Mowgli, Anansi the Spider, and finally, Peter Pan. Grace seems to leap off the page in a succession of expressively detailed watercolors

done in vivid jewel-like tones. This well designed work is a testament to creativity and the power of the human spirit.

Hort, Lenny. *How Many Stars in the Sky?* Illustrated by James Ransome. Tambourine, 1991. (0-688-10103-8) K - P

When a young boy asks the age old question "How many stars in the sky?" his father takes him on a quiet journey of discovery.

Howard, Elizabeth Fitzgerald. *Aunt Flossie's Hats (And Crab Cakes Later)*. Illustrated by James Ransome. Clarion, 1991. (0-395-54682-6) K - P

Sarah and Susan love to visit their great aunt and look through her boxes and boxes of hats. Every hat contains a memory and Aunt Flossie needs little prompting to relate the tales. The richly colored oil paintings are contained within borders set off by white frames. Aunt Flossie's crisp dialogue evokes a sense of the past as she entertains and delights her young audience.

Isadora, Rachel. *At the Crossroads*. Greenwillow, 1991. (0-688-05270-3) P - I

Three small children in a South African village know that this is the day their father is coming home from ten months working in the mines. After school they rush to the crossroads to greet him. The atmosphere is festive at first, but the music and exuberance fade as the wait extends into the night. The cheerfulness of the children is contrasted with the poor living conditions and underscores the harsh reality of this segregated society.

Johnson, Angela. *One of Three*. Illustrated by David Soman. Orchard, 1991. (0-531-05955-3) K - P

A small girl enjoys being the youngest of three sisters. She is one of three who walk to school together, shop together, and play together. When the two older girls go out without her, she discovers that being alone with her parents is a different kind of threesome. The brief text combined with the soft watercolor paintings convey a feeling of family warmth and caring.

Johnson, Angela. *When I Am Old With You*. Illustrated by David Soman. Orchard, 1990. (0-531-05884-0) K - P

A small girl plans with her grandfather the things they will do when both of them are old. The closeness of their relationship and the accuracy of her predictions poignantly underline her ignorance of the knowledge that they can never be old together.

Joose, Barbara M. *Mama, Do You Love Me?* Illustrated by Barbara Lavallee. Chronicle, 1991. (0-87701-759-X) K - P

Set in the Arctic region, a young girl who is a "carbon copy" of her mother, asks repeatedly "Mama, do you love me?" After much reassurance, the young girl adds conditions to her questions, "but, what if...." and always she is assured that mama will still love her—no matter what. Beautifully illustrated, plus a glossary of Arctic animals which enhance the questions in the storyline.

Keegan, Marcia. *Pueblo Boy: Growing Up in Two Worlds*. Cobblehill, 1991. (0-525-65060-1) K - P - I

Timmy Roybal, a ten-year-old Pueblo Indian living in New Mexico, is proud of his heritage. He is shown in some of his daily activities at home and school and as he takes part in the cultural life of the San Ildefonso Pueblo. The text is accompanied by dramatic, color photographs which celebrate the natural beauty of the American Southwest and document the traditional homes of American Indian tribes.

Lankford, Mary D. *Hopscotch Around the World*. Illustrated by Karen Milone. Morrow, 1992. (0-688-08419-2) K - P - I

As Lankford points out, the street game known as hopscotch is as old as human history and as varied in form as the many countries in which it is played to this day. Thus begins her descriptions of 19 hopscotch variations from regions throughout the world. Included in each description are the native name for the game, an explanation of the name's significance, step-by-step directions for playing it, and a descriptive illustration of children in action.

Lewis, Barbara A. *The Kid's Guide to Social Action: How to Solve the Social Problems You Choose and Turn Creative Thinking into Positive Action.* Free Spirit Publishing, 1991. (0-915793-29-6) I - J

> This guide develops the premise that each individual can take positive, informed action to help solve community problems. After describing some of these problems, the author discusses a number of strategies, such as lobbying, fundraising, and cooperative problem solving, that can be used to deal with them.

Livo, Norma J. and Cha, Dia. *Folk Stories of the Hmong: Peoples of Laos, Cambodia and Vietnam.* Libraries Unlimited, 1991. (0-87287-854-6)
J - S - Professional

> Stories and art work from the peoples of these countries help Hmong students reflect a pride in their heritage. The stories are designed to reflect traditional beliefs and customs in such areas as animal symbols, marriage, birth, and death. This book is most helpful for those unfamiliar with the Hmong ways.

McKissack, Patricia and Fredrick McKissack. *A Long Hard Journey: The Story of the Pullman Porter.* Walker, 1989. (0-8027-6884-9) I - J - S

> In this candid chronicle of the Pullman porters' struggle for more humane working conditions, the McKissacks use their story-telling powers to explore the nature of courage, protest, and perseverance. Despite the odds, the Brotherhood of Sleeping Car Porters, formed in 1925 under the tireless leadership of A. Philip Randolph, endured to become the first African American union to win an equitable settlement with a major corporation. The Brotherhood's successful campaign is a vivid reminder of the energy and determination that are needed to bring about social change.

McKissack, Patricia. *A Million Fish—More or Less.* Illustrated by Dena Schutzer. Knopf, 1992. (0-679-80692-X) K - P - I

> This lively tale is destined to be a storytelling classic. Little Hugh Thomas is enthralled by his grandfather's accounts of the Bayou Clapateaux. When he ventures out fishing into the bayou, he discovers the truth of the tales for himself by catching a million fish—more or less.

Medearis, Angela Shelf. *Dancing With the Indians*. Illustrated by Samuel Byrd. Holiday House, 1991. (0-8234-0093-0) K - P - I

The author's inspiration for this story stems from the experiences of her great-grandfather who escaped from slavery and joined a Seminole tribe in Oklahoma. This is a unique story of the intermingling of two cultures.

Myers, Walter Dean. *Now Is Your Time: The African-American Struggle for Freedom*. HarperCollins, 1991. (0-06-024370-8) J - S

The history of African Americans is told through individual stories beginning in 1619 and continuing through the Civil War, the civil rights movement, and into present times. Each person's tale is recounted from the point of view that this experience shaped and developed America today. This is history, fascinatingly told.

Osofsky, Audrey. *Dreamcatcher*. Illustrated by Ed Young. Orchard, 1992. (0-531-05988-X) K - P I

Wrapped in doeskin and snug on a cradleboard on its mother's back, an Ojibway baby sleeps. Protected by a dream net, the infant dreams of dancing, running through fields of silken grass, and playing hide and seek with a butterfly. Nature is an integral part of both the rhythmic tale and the softly colored, strikingly expressive illustrations.

Pijoan, Teresa, collector and reteller. *White Wolf Woman: And Other Native American Transformation Myths*. August House, 1992. (0-87483-201-2) J - S - Professional

Pijoan, a storyteller, has gathered together more than 40 myths from over 30 Native American nations and tribes including the Algonquin, Cherokee, Chiricahua Apache, Hopi, Zuni, Iroquois, Eskimo, Seneca, and Nass River People. The common thread in each of these myths is the power shared by chosen heroes and heroines to transform themselves into animals or objects.

Polacco, Patricia. *Chicken Sunday*. Philomel, 1992. (0-399-22133-6) K- P

Although they come from different backgrounds, three children find a common ground in their desire to buy a special hat for

Miss Eula, a much-loved grandmother who almost always makes them fried chicken for Sunday dinner. The spunky narrator calls on her Russian heritage to solve the predicament which she and her African American playmates confront.

Ringgold, Faith. *Tar Beach*. Crown, 1991. (0-517-58030-6) K - P

While Cassie's family picnics high atop their Harlem apartment building, the little girl dreams of flying over the city and freeing her parents from worry.

Scott, Ann Herbert. *On Mother's Lap*. Illustrated by Glo Coalson. Clarion, 1992. (0-395-58920-7) K

As a young Eskimo boy rocks in his mother's lap, he brings a succession of his favorite belongings including Dolly, Boat, Puppy and his reindeer blanket. When his baby sister wants to join them, he suddenly feels there is no more room. This reissue of the 1972 picture book has new softly colored illustrations which depict the loving relationship between mother and child.

Smalls-Hector, Irene. *Irene and the Big, Fine Nickel*. Illustrated by Tyrone Geter. Little, Brown, 1991. (0-316-79871-1) K - P

As Irene wakes up, so does her Harlem neighborhood. This picture book is a celebration of everyday living as shown in family, friends and community. The softly textured paintings place vibrant figures on a muted background. Through words and pictures, the setting becomes an integral part of the work which reflects the African American culture of the 1950s.

Stolz, Mary. *Storm in the Night*. Illustrated by Pat Cummings. Harper and Row, 1988. (0-06-025912-4) K - P

Thomas is uneasy when the power goes off and the only illumination comes from streaks of lightning. He sits on the porch and listens to his grandfather tell a story about his own childhood fear of storms. The lyrical text tells of sounds, memories and apprehensions, while the luminous illustrations portray the magic of a summer storm and the strong relationship between Thomas and his grandfather.

Taylor, Mildred D. *The Gold Cadillac*. Illustrated by Michael Hays. Dial, 1991. (0-8037-0342-2) I

Wilma and 'lois are as excited about their father's new gold Cadillac as they are puzzled by their mother's refusal to ride in it. Things become even more complicated when the family sets out from Ohio to Mississippi to visit their relatives. For the first time the girls become aware of racial prejudice and the fear that accompanies it. The author's extraordinary use of language creates a powerful and moving account of strength and courage in the face of injustice.

Thomas, Joyce Carol. *Marked by Fire*. Avon, 1982. (0-380-79327-X) J - S

At birth Abyssinia is seared by a burning coal, marking her physically and spiritually to bear the honor and burden of becoming a healer and midwife for her people. Abandoned by her father, raped by a neighbor and besieged by a deranged neighbor, she is healed by loving glances and nourishing greens, crackling corn bread, cakes and cobblers. Thomas takes us into a community of caring elders who help Abby survive her many trials.

Thomson, Peggy. *City Kids in China*. Illustrated by Paul S. Conklin. Harper and Row, 1991. (0-06-021654-9) J

With the help of abundant black and white action photographs, the author brings to life neighborhoods, dwellings, shops, markets, and schools in the contemporary industrial city of Changsha. Equipped with the journalist's eye for detail and nuance and the anthropologist's curiosity about the habits, traditions, attitudes, and politics of a people, she recreates a world by focusing on the particulars of family life, medicinal practices, long-standing customs, the formidable Chinese language, and a gruelling educational system. Unfortunately, she glosses over the repercussions of China's repressive government.

Uchida, Yoshiko. *The Best Bad Thing*. Margaret K. McElderry, 1983. (0-689-50290-7) I

Rinko is unhappy when her parents volunteer her to help one of their friends. Mrs. Hata's husband has died and she is struggling to manage her farm and two small sons. A series of "bad happenings" seem to confirm her fears, until she discovers that things are not always what they seem. There is a strong sense of family and community in the fast-paced, well-crafted story narrated by this spirited Japanese heroine.

Walker, Barbara A. *Laughing Together: Giggles and Grins from Around the Globe*. Illustrated by Simms Tabak. Free Spirit Publishing, 1992. (0-915793-37-7) P - I

Tongue twisters, riddles, jokes, jump rope and counting-out rhymes, nonsense verse, and other grin-provoking, contagiously rhythmic, upbeat forms of language play, many of them in their original language alongside an English translation, transport us to over one hundred countries. A book to use on short and long trips and to pass around. This serves as a natural catalyst for further exploration of the cultures represented.

Walter, Mildred Pitts. *Justin and the Best Biscuits in the World*. Illustrated by Catherine Stock. Lothrop, Lee & Shepard, 1986. (0-688-06645-3) P - I

After his father's death, Justin lives with his mother and two older sisters. It seems they are always fussing at him and expecting him to do "women's work." During a summer visit with Grandpa, Justin is surprised to find that his grandfather is an excellent housekeeper as well as a capable rancher. Grandpa wins a blue ribbon for his biscuits and Justin gains a new appreciation for a job well done. The author gives a sensitive portrayal of the conflicts of a young boy growing up in a female oriented household,

Watts, Irene N. *Just a Minute*. Heinemann Educational Books, 1990. Professional

The ten plays in this collection are adaptations of folktales and legends that address timeless, universal themes and issues such as greed (*The Talking Fish*), honesty (*The Captive Moon*), deception (*The Pied Piper of Hamelin*), loyalty (*Sungold*), and discrimination (*The Enchanted Spring*). Designed to be staged in any space, each play is accompanied by activities that stimulate involvement through improvisation, pantomime, movement, discussion, and related reading. An inventive introduction to play reading, play performing, and the basic elements of stories steeped in the unpretentious wisdom of the oral tradition.

West, John O. *Mexican-American Folklore*. August House, 1988. (0-87483-059-1) Professional

Drawing upon the folkways of three cultures—Indian, Spanish, and Mexican—West offers an entertaining and enlightening potpourri of traditional literature, including proverbs, riddles, folksongs, and enticing narratives, and everyday folklore such as children's games, foods, crafts, dress and customs.

Williams, Vera B. *More, More, More Said the Baby*. Greenwillow, 1990. (0-688-09173-3) K - P

Multi-racial illustrations in this picture book become a powerful teaching tool for the young. Three infants from different cultures are shown separately in the daily activities common to all, thus reinforcing the universality of family life.

Woodson, Jacqueline. *Last Summer With Maizon*. Doubleday, 1990. (0-385-30045-X) I

This is the story of Margaret's first, intense experience with the kind of unbearable pain that nudges her out of childhood. It tells of how she survives her father's death and how she copes when Maizon, her talented best friend in whose shadow she lives, leaves their close-knit Brooklyn neighborhood to attend an exclusive boarding school. Margaret's slow, tentative emergence into self-awareness begins when she recognizes and acknowledges her own special talents.

Yee, Paul. *Tales from Gold Mountain: Stories of the Chinese in the New World*. Illustrated by Simon Ng. Macmillan, 1990. (0-02-793621-X) J
The experiences of early Chinese immigrants to Canada are captured in compelling fantasies that draw on the folk traditions of southern China. Simon Ng's dream-like illustrations enrich tales that depict the hardships and the triumphs of astonishingly resourceful and resilient people.

APPENDIX B

SOURCES OF MULTICULTURAL MATERIALS

Adoptive Families of America

3333 Hwy., 100N
Minneapolis, MN 55422
(612) 533-4829

A national nonprofit membership organization of 15,000 families and individuals, and over 250 adoptive parent support groups which provides problem-solving assistance and information about the challenges of adoption to members and prospective adoptive families.

Afro-Am, Inc.

819 South Wabash Avenue, Suite 610
Chicago, IL 60605

A catalog offering African American materials and other multi-ethnic materials such as books, toys, teaching aids, posters, plays, videos, and more.

Annick Press

15 Patricia Avenue
Willowdale, Ontario
Canada M2M 1H9

A Canadian publishing company dedicated exclusively to children's literature. Their books portray children as capable and imaginative persons who use good judgement.

Arte Publico Press

The Americas Review
University of Houston
Houston, TX 77204-2090

The oldest and largest publisher of Hispanic literature in the United States providing books of fiction, poetry, literary criticism, and children's literature by the leading figures of Mexican American, Puerto Rican and Cuban cultures. Especially focuses on Hispanic women's literature.

A.R.T.S. (Art Resources for Teachers and Students, Inc.)

32 Market Street
New York, NY 10002

A nonprofit resource center which works with Chinese and Hispanic youth on New York's lower East Side, transcending the culture of their own communities and that of the African American, Jewish and Italian neighborhoods. A number of booklet publications are available.

Asia Resource Center

P.O. Box 15275
Washington, D.C. 20003
(202) 547-1114

Provides educational resources on the peoples and cultures of Asia. Materials deal with issues of human rights, abuse, nuclear disarmament, justice for the poor, and the rights of women and minorities and are available in the form of videos, slide shows, books, speakers, exhibits, subscriptions, and special programs.

Brown Sugar and Spice

8584 Whitehorn
Romulus, MI 48174

A distributor for an assortment of educational African American materials.

Carolina Wren Press

P.O. Box 277
Carrboro, NC 27510
(919) 560-2738

Office address: 120 Morris St.
Durham, NC 27701

A collection of fiction, poetry, drama, nonfiction, and nonsexist multicultural children's books.

Charhill Publishers

4468 San Francisco Ave.
P.O. Box 150124
St. Louis, MO 63115
(314) 382-4998

Producer of learning aids particularly for African American children. A major focus is "Wee Folks," a phonetic approach to beginning reading (five books each focusing on different levels of reading).

Children's Book Press

1461 Ninth Ave.
San Francisco, CA 94122
(415) 655-3395

A source for award winning multicultural children's books and audiocassettes.

China Books and Periodicals

2929 Twenty-fourth St.
San Francisco, CA 94110

A seasonal offering of books about Chinese culture, also featuring music on compact disc, software for learning and writing Chinese, greeting cards, maps, and videos.

Cobblestone Publishing, Inc.

30 Grove Street
St. Petersburg, NH 03458

The publisher of four in-depth children's magazines, each with a particular emphasis: *Faces* / Multicultural Studies; *Cobblestone* /

The History Magazine for Young People; *Calliope* / Magazine of World History; and *Odyssey* / Astronomy and Space Exploration. Individual back issues are available as are some theme packs featuring several related back issues, such as Native Americans.

Community Graphics

San Francisco Study Center
1095 Market St., Room 602
San Francisco, CA 94103
(415) 626-1650

A source for educational materials such as curriculum guides, essays, slide shows, cassettes, and classroom sets (children's books, cassette, and teacher's guide). These materials can be used as supplemental materials to an existing school curriculum.

Crestwood Company

Communication Aids for Children and Adults
6625 N. Sidney Place
Milwaukee, WI 53209-3259

A variety of communication aids for children and adults including stickers, porta-boards, listen-aiders (for people with hearing loss), and talking boards.

Daybreak Star Press

P.O. Box 99100
Seattle, WA 98199

A wide selection of educational materials on Native Americans, including the *Daybreak Star Indian Reader*, a 24 page learning resource for children in the elementary grades. Features culturally focused articles and activities appropriate for students in grades 4-6.

Desmond A. Reid Enterprises (D.A.R.E.)

Multicultural Books
(Quality Books and Educational Supplies)
P.O. Box 1168
Brooklyn, NY 11202

Offers African American literature, prose, educational resources (such as cookbooks), fashion, encyclopedias, and history for children, teens, young adults and teachers.

Education Equity Concepts, Inc.

114 E. 32nd St.
New York, NY 10016

A national, nonprofit organization to foster equal educational opportunity. The designer of innovative programs and materials to help eliminate sex, race, and disability bias.

Educational Record Center, Inc.

Building 400, Suite 400
1575 Northside Drive., N. W.
Atlanta, GA 30318-4298
(404) 352-8282
(800) 438-1637

Provides a wide selection of audiovisual materials including read-alongs, videos, filmstrips, compact discs, phonodiscs, and cassettes.

Enslow Publishers, Inc.

Bloy Street and Ramsey Avenue
P.O. Box 777
Hillside, NJ 97205-0777

Publishers of resources for elementary and secondary education including a wide variety of multicultural related themes such as, Great African Americans, books for beginning readers on aspiring African Americans who made a difference and Issues in Focus, considers the pros & cons of important issues.

The Greenfield Review Press

Native American Authors Distribution Project
2 Middle Grove Road
P.O. Box 308
Greenfield Center, NY 12833

Specializing in books by Native American writers and offering over 250 titles from over seventy publishers. Includes novels, books of poetry, children's literature, journals, newspapers, how-to, history, and cassette tapes of Native American storytelling.

Heian International

1260 Pacific Street
P.O. Box 1013
Union City, CA 94587

A seasonal offering of Asian resources including arts and crafts, Asian culture, children's books, astrology, cooking, literature, travel, language, dictionaries, and Asian calendars.

The Heritage Key, Inc.

10116 Scoville Ave.
Sunland, CA 91040

Multicultural resources such as, books, dolls, games, maps, videos, and display materials

The Institute for Peace and Justice

4144 Lindell Avenue., #122
St. Louis, MO 63108
(314) 533-4445

Publishes a resource catalog of peace/justice materials and a bibliography of children's books and cassettes with a theme of multiculturalism and peace/conflict resolution.

Intercultural Press, Inc.

P.O. Box 700
Yarmouth, ME 04096
(207) 846-5168

A publisher of international and multicultural materials for adults, but also for use as resources or reference materials for schools.

The Interracial Family Circle

P.O. Box 53290
Washington, D.C. 20009

An organization of interracial families which offers members a chance to socialize with other interracial families. Serves to educate both themselves and the publica about interracial and intercultural families.

Kar-Ben

6800 Tildenwood Lane
Rockville, MD 20852
(301)984-8733
1-800-4-KARBEN

Books of a variety of themes for and about Jewish children such as Jewish holidays, food, customs, and stories.

Medical Toys and Books

Pediatric Projects, Inc.
Box 1880
Santa Monica, CA 90406-9920

Some multicultural materials, including books, disabled and anatomically correct dolls.

Multicultural Publishers Exchange

P.O. Box 9869
Madison, WI 53715
(608) 244-5633

The only active association for book publishers of color. Provides an extensive list of multicultural offerings for children and older audiences.

The Multifunctional Resource Center

310 Eighth Street, Suite 220
Oakland, CA 94607

Publishes a resource guide to bilingual education for new immigrant and refugee LEP students. Included are books about educational concerns, films and videos about Southeastern Asians, and lists of resource agencies.

Music for Little People

Box 1460
Redway, CA 95560

A distributor of an enormous selection of children's audio, video, and educational entertainment products.

National Women's History Project

7738 Bell Road
Windsor, CA 95492-8518
(707) 838-6000

An extensive resource for information on women and their history: posters, women's history month celebration supplies, gifts, books, videos, display items, and classroom materials.

New Day Press

c/o Karamu House
2355 E. 89th St.
Cleveland, OH 44106
(216) 795-7070

Publishers of several books related to the history of African Americans in Ohio.

New Seed Press

P.O. Box 9488
Berkley, CA 94709-0488

Publishers of children's books free from stereotyping which portray people living in various situations and which encourage thinking about how the world could be different.

OYATE

2702 Mathews St.
Berkley, CA 94702
(510)848-6700

A nonprofit organization of Native and Métis Elders, artists, activists, educators, and writers who have come together to bring the real histories of the indigenous people of this continent to the attention of all Americans. Children's books and materials written and illustrated by Native people are included among the materials they distribute.

Positive Images

301 G. Street, S.W. 329
Washington, D.C. 22024

Specializes in Afrocentric children's books, games, and videos in addition to offering a selection for adults and educators.

Pueblo to People

2105 Silber Road, Suite 101
Houston, TX 77055
(800) 843-5257

A nonprofit organization founded in 1979 which focuses efforts on craft and agricultural cooperatives of very low income people in Latin America. A varied selection of clothing, art, posters, cards, craft items, pottery, and other realia is available.

Red and Black Books

432 15th Ave., E.
Seattle, WA 98112
(206) 322-READ

Provides a list of multicultural materials and resources about children's issues, some which deal with racism and sexism. Red and Black Books is an independent bookstore which makes available materials that promote self-esteem in children of all backgrounds, increase intercultural understanding, and foster awareness of the interdependence of life on earth.

Redleaf Press

450 North Syndicate, Suite 5
St. Paul, MN 55104-4125

Publishes *Roots and Wings*, a new approach to multicultural education which gives children the support of being rooted in their culture and the strength to soar beyond prejudice and discrimination. Redleaf Press serves as a source for materials for early childhood educators.

Silo

P.O. Box 429
Waterbury, VT 05676
(802) 244-5178

A source for "Silo's World Music Collection: Alternative Recordings," a catalog whose features range from field recordings of authentic ethnic music from around the world to sophisticated blends of music styles drawn from a variety of cultures.

Smithsonian / Folkways Recordings

416 Hungerford Dr., Suite 320
Rockville, MD 20850

A collection of over 2100 historic folk recordings listed by performer, geographic area, and subject matter.

Syracuse Cultural Workers

P.O. Box 6367
Syracuse, NY 13217

An assortment of multicultural and global awareness materials and art including posters, calendars, t-shirts, bags, cards, books, flags, buttons, and bumper stickers.

Third World Press

7524 S. Cottage Grove
P.O. Box 730
Chicago, IL 60619
(312) 651-0700

The nation's oldest, continuous African American owned publishing company which publishes books in all genres.

U.S. Committee for UNICEF

333 E. 38th St.
New York, NY 10016

Publishes a guide to global cultural heritage through the use of folk tales, maps, and activities: "Folktales and Stories: An Elementary Student's Passport to the World."

Victory Publishing
3504 Oak Drive
Menlo Park, CA 94025

Publishes educational materials appropriate for learning Spanish in grades K-6 such as *Antologia de Poesía,* a collection of poetry suggested for teaching literature and reading to children.

APPENDIX C

VIRGINIA HAMILTON MANUSCRIPT COLLECTION

BY ALEX GILDZEN

"An Inventory of the Virginia Hamilton Papers at the Kent State University Libraries"

The Kent State University Libraries established a Department of Special Collections in 1969. From the beginning children's literature was a cornerstone of the department. One of its first acquisitions was a collection devoted to *Alice in Wonderland*. As the department grew, its holdings came to include the papers of Cynthia Rylant, original drawings by Randolph Caldecott and Margaret Ayer, letters from Kate Greenaway, Lois Lenski and Jean Bothwell, the first issue of the *Superman* comic book, the manuscript of Jacqueline Jackson's *The Taste of Spruce Gum* (1966), the Roy VanDevier collection of juvenile series, the Clara O. Jackson collection of international children's books and the archives of the Saalfield Publishing Company with its vast collection of mint condition activity books, paperdolls and coloring books.

In April 1985, Virginia Hamilton gave the first lecture established at Kent State University in her name. She concluded her remarks with the announcement that she would deposit her papers at Kent. The first manuscripts arrived in January 1986 and were officially presented by the author at a reception in the Special Collections reading room during the second annual conference in April. To coincide with the sixth annual conference the department mounted a major exhibition of the Virginia Hamilton papers.

The following description of the papers on deposit as of May 1992 follows the publication order of the books.

Paul Robeson: The Life And Times of a Free Black Man

1st draft—Incomplete typescript with holograph revisions and suggestions from the editor.

Working draft—Primarily a photocopy with typescript interspersed; heavily annotated.

Copy edited ms.—Typescript of 210 pages plus foreword and afterword materials.

Master proof—Corrected galleys–July 1974.

Page proof—Author's "courtesy set"–22 August 1974.

M.C. Higgins, the Great

Early draft, fragment—Includes comments from Hamilton's editor, Susan Hirschman.

Original draft—Includes material not in finished work.

Original fragments, rewrites—Typescript of chapters 1–8 followed by a photocopy of chapters 9–14, an earlier typescript of chapters 9–14 and a photocopy of complete manuscript.

Final ms. sent to publisher—The author's photocopy.

Copy edited ms.—Typescript of 277 pages.

Author's galleys —Master set (4 February 1974), and the author's copy.

Script—Photocopy of first half of the script for the Miller Brody filmstrip/cassette.

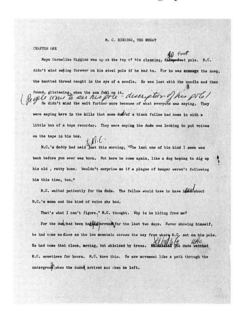

M. C. Higgins, the Great. Typescript from chapter one.

Arilla Sun Down

Early draft, fragment—Includes typescript of chapter 10, carbon of "Notes," and miscellaneous source material.

Copy edited ms.—Typescript pf 267 pages.

Galley proofs—"Reader's Set."

Justice and Her Brothers

Very young drafts—Includes the beginning of the book under an earlier title, "The Great Snake Race."

Original photocopy—270 pages, with the title "Three."

Second original, rewrite—Photocopy interspersed with carbons of rewritten pages.

Draft photocopy with holograph corrections— Book still called "Three."

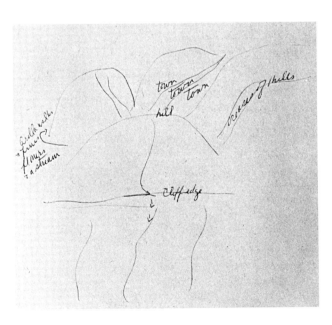

Arilla Sun Down. Early sketch of setting by Virginia Hamilton.

Copy edited ms.—Typescript of 241 pages.
Galley proofs—Two sets.

Dustland

Early rewrites—Corrected typescripts of chapters two and three.

Copy edited ms.—Typescript of 186 pages. Galley proofs, incomplete set.

Letter from editor T.L.S., commenting on manuscript (10 July 1979), accompanied by two pages of holograph and typed draft responses from Hamilton.

The Gathering

Original corrected photocopy of 203 pages.
Galley proofs with minor corrections.

The Magical Adventures of Pretty Pearl

Early original ms.—Typescript of 223 pages with photocopies of revised pages.

"Ms.,processing— Typescript revised by both author and editor.

Galley proofs—Two master sets: "1st pass" (4 January 1983) and "2nd pass" (19 January 1983).

A Little Love

Original corrected photocopy under earlier title, "Sheema, Queen of the Road."

Proofs corrected—Master set of galleys (20 February 1984) and corrected master set of page proofs (27 March 1984).

Junius Over Far

Original ms.—Typescript of 269 pages with editor's queries and author's corrections.

Galley proofs—Corrected master set (17 December 1984) and corrected revised set (23 January 1985).

Original dummy—Corrected (21 February 1985).

A White Romance

Original draft—Partial typescript of early versions, accompanied by photocopy of T.L.S. from Hamilton to her

editors at Philomel Books
(31 December 1986).

Final ms.—Corrected typescript of 134 pages.

Draft—Corrected photocopy of 213 pages.

Galley proofs—Corrected galleys, accompanied by a bound set, uncorrected proof for limited distribution.

The Mystery of Drear House

Early fragment—Typescript of 116 pages under earlier title, "The Secret of Pluto's Cave," accompanied by "Working-out of Plot," a drawing of "Rough Layout of Drear House, Hillside, Pluto's Cave," A.L.S. from Hamilton to her editor Susan Hirschman (7 July 1984) and fragments written in Puerto Rico in 1985.

Very early draft—Corrected typescript of 239 pages.

1st Submission—Photocopy of 278 pages.

Final submission—Photocopy of 213 pages.

Final ms.—Photocopy of 213 pages (11 March 1986), accompanied by photocopy of T.L.S. from Hamilton to Hirschman (1 March 1986).

Anthony Burns: The Defeat and Triumph of a Fugitive Slave

Original ms.—Photocopy of 116 pages under first title, "The Anthony Burns Rescue Case."

Original fragments—Corrected typescript under earlier title, "The Rescue of Anthony Burns."

Early original—Corrected typescript of 210 pages, accompanied by another copy with the title "The Rescue of Anthony Burns," identified by the author as "Final ms. with revisions."

Revised ms.—Typescript reviewed by editor with title, "The Fugitive, Anthony Burns: The Defeat and Triumph of a Slave."

Revisions and cuts—A list of characters, "outtakes" from the original manuscript and revisions.

Letters to editor—Copies of T.L.S. from Hamilton to her editor Stephanie Spinner (15 June 1987, 12 October 1987) and three pages of notes.

Copy edited ms.—Photocopy of 169 pages, accompanied by T.L.S. to Hamilton from Spinner (21 December 1987).

Galley proofs—Dated 23 January 1988.

CONTRIBUTOR S
NOTE

Alex Gildzen, curator of Special Collections and Archives at the Kent State University Libraries, is the author of *The Avalanche of Time: Selected Poems 1964-1984*, co-author of *Joseph Chaikin: A Bio-Bibliography* and co-editor of the anthology *A Gathering of Poets*.

INDEX